WILDLIFE OF C

BRITISH ISLES

TONY SOPER

ILLUSTRATIONS BY
DAN POWELL

Bradt Travel Guides, UK
The Globe Pequot Press Inc, USA

Published in 2002 by Bradt Travel Guides Ltd.
19 High Street, Chalfont St Peter, Bucks SL9 9QE, England
Published in the USA by The Globe Pequot Press Inc,
246 Goose Lane, PO Box 480, Guilford, Connecticut 06437-0480

Text copyright © 2002 Tony Soper
Illustrations copyright © 2002 Dan Powell
Map copyright © 2002 Bradt Travel Guides Ltd

British Library Cataloguing-in-Publication Data
A catalogue record for this book is available from the British Library

ISBN 1 84162 058 0

Library of Congress Cataloging-in-Publication Data applied for

Front cover Puffins at sea
(Dan Powell)
Map Alan Whitaker

Typeset from the author's disc by Concise Artisans
Printed and bound in Italy by Printer Trento

CONTENTS

MAJOR SEABIRD BREEDING STATIONS

Herma Ness
Superb cliffs, gannet stacks, puffins, guillemots, skuas.

Shetland Is.

Sule Skerry
Gannets, puffins.

Noss
Steep cliffs; thousands of gannets, fulmars, auks, skuas, kittiwakes.

North Rona
Gannets, auks, fulmars, skuas.

Sula Sgeir
Massive gannetry, exploited annually on a sustainable basis by the men of Lewis.

Orkney Is

Fair Isle
World-famous bird observatory, primarily for migration study. Skuas, fulmars, storm petrels, puffins, black guillemots. NTS

Flannan Is
Gannets, auks, gulls etc.

Outer Hebrides

Handa
Thousands of seabirds, including rock doves, great and Arctic skuas, red-throated divers. SWT

St Kilda
Sensational gannet stacks, world-class seabird cliffs. NTS

Skye

Shiant Is
Miniature St Kilda, without gannets. Abundant razorbills, possible sea eagles.

North Sea

Atlantic

Fowlesheugh
Large colonies auks, kittiwakes, some fulmars, shags. RSPB

Scotland

Isle of May
Spectacular cliff colonies, plenty of puffins, terns. SNH

Rathlin Is
Superb auk stacks, bird cliffs. RSPB

Farne Is
Auks, kittiwakes, fulmars, shags, eiders, terns. NT

Ocean

N

Bradt

Northern Ireland

Bempton
Spectacular chalk cliffs, ledges swarming with auks, fulmars, gulls: only mainland colony of gannets. RSPB

IRISH

Irish Sea

REPUBLIC

Bardsey
Bird observatory, mainly for migration studies. Shags, auks, gulls. BIT

The Skelligs
Large colony gannets, shearwaters, storm petrels, puffins.

Wales   *England*

Skomer
Perfect seabird island. Thousands of auks, Manx shearwaters, gulls, peregrines, choughs etc. WWWT

Great Saltee
Gannets, petrels, auks.

Grassholm
Gannet stronghold. RSPB

Skokholm
First British bird observatory. Auks, shearwaters, petrels. WWWT

Cape Clear Is
Bird observatory since 1959. Outstanding seawatch station.

Lundy
Beautiful, but not major seabird breeding site. NT

St Agnes
Famous for exotic migrants in October; fair presence of breeding seabirds.

Alderney
Gannetry at Ortac.

English Channel

FRANCE

KEY

⤳	Major seabird breeding station
BIT	Bardsey Island Trust
NT	National Trust
RSPB	Royal Society for the Protection of Birds
SNH	Scottish National Heritage
NTS	National Trust for Scotland
SWT	Scottish Wildlife Trust
WWWT	West Wales Wildlife Trust

0	50km
0	35 mile

INTRODUCTION

'The use of the sea and air is common to all people; neither can a title to the ocean belong to any people or private persons, for as much as neither nature nor public use and custom permit any possession thereof.'

Queen Elizabeth I of England

Coasting the inshore waters of these islands offers the most enjoyable way to sample our rich, seagoing wildlife. Great whales pass close by on their migrations, lesser whales fish the Minch and the coast of Wales and the Western Approaches. If you're lucky, dolphins will cavort in your bow wave and gannets plunge for mackerel in your wake. Grey seals patronise the remotest caves and beaches while common seals haul out and pup on tidal sandbanks. As for seabirds, the coast and islands of Britain and Ireland host a significant part of the world's populations, and they fish our seas, albeit in uneasy harmony with fishermen. Sail the Channel in summer and you are highly likely to be joined by a racing pigeon  which is thinking of giving up racing to go hippy on the cliffs. You may pass an off-duty puffin; you may close on a turtle making a meal of a giant jellyfish.

On a foul day with biting wind and monstrous waves there may be a storm-petrel to keep you company; on a sunny day with a soldier's wind there will be kittiwakes and fulmars to bring extra life to the scene. But a set of reference books with information about all the species you're likely to meet would seriously overflow your shelf space. This slim volume aims to provide enough to keep you going till you're back ashore to a decent library!

TAXONOMY, OR WHAT'S IN A NAME?

Eider to some, cuddy duck to others and *eidereend* to a Dutchman, but *Somateria mollissima* all over the world! The value of scientific names is that being based on a dead language – Latin – they are not subject to the sort of changes brought about by time and common usage, which gives words different meanings in different decades. The value of an ossified language is beyond price to the taxonomist who catalogues living creatures.

Scientists and philosophers struggled for centuries to devise a practical filing system for classifying the natural world. It was in 1735 that the Swedish naturalist Linnaeus published his watershed work Systema Naturae, which established the biological principles for listing plants and animals. His principle was to list into ever smaller groupings those plants or animals which displayed similarities with each other.

Working from the top, he proposed plant and animal Kingdoms. Then, he divided the animals (everything from elephants to sandhoppers) into Phyla, one of which encompasses the vertebrates (animals with backbones). This Phylum Chordata, as it is known, is further divided into a number of Classes, one of which is for mammals, where we ourselves are placed, another of which is for birds, the Class of Aves. Twenty-six Orders of birds yet again sub-divide into Families, and within the Families a group of closely related birds with common traits of behaviour or plumage or structure represent a Genus, which is finally divided into Species, the 'kinds' of bird.

In this way, a bird is known by its generic name suffixed by its specific name. The puffin *Fratercula arctica*, for example, belongs to the auk Family (Alcidae) which is part of the Charadriiformes Order of the bird Class of the vertebrate branch of the Animal Kingdom. So, a puffin from root to blossom:

Kingdom	Animalia
Phylum	Chordata
Class	Aves
Order	CHARADRIIFORMES
Family	ALCIDAE
Genus	FRATERCULA
Species	*Fratercula arctica*

There are further divisions into subphyla, sub and super families, and subspecies, but the binomial system which gives most species a name comprising two words seems quite enough to be going on with…

THE ECONOMY OF THE SEA

Many millions of creatures live there, yet on rare days of glassy calm the sea may look featureless, flat and lifeless to a casual observer. On wild, wet and frightening days it may still seem superficially barren. But appearances are deceptive, and the winds which whip the surface into such varied responses also power the currents which provide the key to unlocking a cornucopia of food that supports unimaginable quantities of life.

The quantity of food available to sea-going wildlife relates to the concentrations of nutrients in upwelling waters. For these nutrients, along with the power of the sun's light and the warmth of the sea, are the raw materials which are taken up by microscopic plants like diatoms in the free-floating phytoplankton. In turn the surface 'meadows' of plankton plants are 'grazed' by copepods and a myriad of other zooplankton animals.

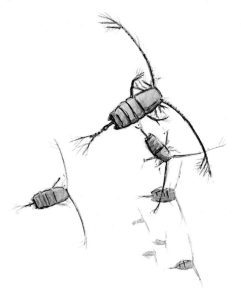

For sheer abundance, copepods rule the world; they are the most important link in the marine food chain, eaten by almost everything, from fish to birds to whales. With antennae at the bow and a tail at the stern, they progress in a stately fashion by paddling with their legs ('kope' in Greek means 'oar', so copepod means 'oar-footed').

The fact that a very large percentage of the plankton is eaten by something larger is no accident; it is part of the fundamental economy of the sea. An animal larva may eat some of the phytoplankton, only to be eaten itself by a small fish. The fish then forms part of a mackerel's breakfast, and the mackerel is eaten for dinner by a shark, and thus we have a classic 'food chain'. At the top of each food chain comes the biggest predator, say a killer whale, but in due course he too will die and his decaying remains form food for the plankton. Thus the cycle is revitalised.

Sometimes the phytoplankton growth may be so prolific that it imparts a definite colour to the sea, perhaps red or yellow. These plankton blooms – 'red tides' – can have a disastrous effect because their potentially poisonous mineral contents may be concentrated in the animals which eat too much of them. This in turn may cause subsequent distress, or even death, to animals higher up the food chain. Thus seabirds which have eaten molluscs containing high concentrations of toxic dinoflagellates have been found dead on the shore. People who have eaten cockles or mussels affected by the 'red tide' may suffer serious, or even fatal, attacks of food poisoning. The molluscs are apparently unaffected, simply acting as agents for poisons which they pass on to predators.

There are also seasonal forces at work in fuelling the sea's bounty. The major influences, as on land, are the changes in day-length and temperature associated with the solar cycle. In spring the plants multiply and thrive on the extra light, then in summer, triggered by warmth, the animals release their spawn to grow and feed on the rich pasture, so that in summer the zooplankton is in the ascendant. When autumn gales stir up the sea-bed and bring a flush of fresh, nutrient-rich debris to the surface the phytoplankton enjoys a brief extra flowering. Then in winter the period of plenty is over and, as on land, the sea animals face a time of test, only the fittest passing the selection board and surviving to continue their life-cycle. Nevertheless the sea seasons are not so marked as those ashore, and one of the great advantages of a marine existence is that it offers a reasonably stable environment, where temperature change, for instance, is slow. While the hottest days on land may be in June, it is August/September before the sea achieves its greatest warmth, with no wild daily fluctuations.

The plankton plants and animals are at the mercy of tidal currents, but the two other great divisions of life at sea have a certain independence. The nekton comprises all those animals which have the ability to swim, while the benthos are those animals which make their living on the sea-bed, taking advantage of the rain of organic debris that drifts down from the surface regions. Both divisions include animals from different classes, but in each case fish are the most highly and successfully adapted to the aquatic life. Snails and crabs may crawl about the bottom, stay put or even float, but fish can do all theses things, and also enjoy the freedom of the open waters.

So, one way or another there are vast quantities of food in the sea, and clearly that is what has encouraged birds to exploit the marine environment. Some are deep-sea sailors, like fulmars and shearwaters; some are inshore fishermen and longshoremen, like cormorants and most of the gulls. Some, like divers (loons) and grebes, spend only part of the year at sea; others, like sea-ducks, specialise in shallow-water diving. Seabirds are not as diverse a group as those of the land, for of roughly nine thousand kinds of birds only some three hundred or so can be called seabirds. However, they make up for a paucity of species by sheer numbers; occupying an environment which is relatively safe, seabirds live long lives and flourish.

Birds make subtle use of the varying wind draughts associated with waves. They ride the updraught created as wind presses against waves. They can rise above the crest, then soar along the trough using complex energy-differences set up by the friction between the opposing forces of wind and water. In this way they ride the endless waves. And by the same token they will ride the bow and quarter waves set up by the passage of a ship through the sea.

In times of violent weather seabirds will avoid the worst of it whenever possible. They survive hurricanes by getting out of their way. Provided there's plenty of sea room they simply drift to leeward, out of the path of the blow, returning to station when the worst has passed. In a lesser blow, like a gale, they will avoid the worst effects by riding them out in the lee of a continuous wave, flying along in parallel on the sheltered side. For all that, disaster does strike, especially in the case of the smaller and lighter species. Sea-going waders such as phalaropes are especially vulnerable; attempting to ride it out on the surface they may be simply blown into the air. Huge numbers die in storms. Little auks and storm-petrels may be 'wrecked' ashore in great numbers in inclement weather, to be discovered wandering disconsolately around the rain-sodden streets of inland towns, far from the sea.

On the plus side, the great virtue of the sea is that it is a relatively safe place most of the time. There are no foxes and very few people! Fishing activities by man, however, pose a real threat to seabirds, seals and whales. Twenty thousand auks drown in trammel nets in Galway Bay alone each year. Drift nets are said to account for half a million guillemots annually. Remnants of discarded nets may be picked up and taken ashore as nesting material, to trap legs and entangle the necks of gannets. Plastic may strangle seals and turtles.

At different times our coastline has been important to us as a springboard for inland exploration and settlement, for defence, as a base from which to harvest the riches of the sea, a place to colonise for industry and for holiday fun. The emphasis has changed with changing times. It wasn't until the coming of the railways in the middle of the 19th century, for example, that people flocked to the coast for health and recreation, but since that Victorian discovery of the glorious freedom of the seaside the coast and inshore waters have remained as popular as ever. Sailing inshore waters brings us into close contact with the most superbly adapted of all creatures – seafarers.

INVERTEBRATES

Just under the surface, and out of sight, the sea is teeming with life. Millions of tiny plankton plants and animals float and drift in the current, nourished by upwelling minerals and the light and warmth of the sun and providing food for larger creatures. Young fish of all sorts, like herrings and mackerel, hunt the small stuff and are in turn hunted by birds, sharks and whales. There is endless carnage near the surface, and a rain of debris falls on to the sea-bed where bottom-dwellers like crabs, lobsters and flatfish live on this food and on one another. Clouds of spores or eggs rise to enrich the plankton and maintain the cycle. Birds, paddling on the surface or diving out of the sky, scoop or stab the fish. Large creatures feed on smaller ones, but all die eventually, their bodies providing food for others. In the sea, nothing is wasted.

BIOLUMINESCENCE

On a calm, dark night in late summer you may sometimes see one of the most magical performances of nature. The bow wave and the wash of a vessel may sparkle with curious flashes; the water might splash and drip from the oar blades of a dinghy as if on fire; as wavelets lap along the shore their line may be marked by a glow of pale greenish light. All of these phenomena are caused by tiny dinoflagellates such as noctiluca, which are present in the sea in uncountable numbers. When they are agitated or disturbed, they glow with phosphorescence and produce an unforgettable firework display. Ctenophores like the sea gooseberry also exhibit flashes of luminescence at night.

'The vessel drove before her bows two billows of liquid phosphorus, and in her wake she was followed by a milky train. As far as the eye reached, the crest of every wave was bright from the reflected glare of these livid flames.'

Charles Darwin, *Voyage of the Beagle*

JELLYFISH

LION'S MANE JELLYFISH *Cyanea capillata*
Native to British waters, but not common, the lion's mane jellyfish is a gaudy east-coast creature of blue and violet, hung with eight bunches of tentacles. It's around 50cm in diameter, but may be much larger, and is also a severe stinger.

MOON JELLYFISH *Aurelia aurita*
The most common of our jellyfish, around 40cm in diameter, the moon jelly resembles an upside-down saucer with two crossed oval marks, purple-violet in colour, on the upper side of the bell. It does have stinging tentacles but hardly powerful enough to affect human skins. It uses its tentacles to trap small plankton animals like copepods.

COMPASS JELLYFISH *Chrysaora hysoscella*
Measuring anything from 10 to 46cm in diameter, the compass jellyfish is milk-white with an orange-brown central spot and radii, and is found in the south and west of the British Isles.

RHIZOSTOMA *Rhizostoma octopus*
Football-sized or much larger (up to 1m in diameter), and mushroom-shaped, this is the largest jellyfish to reach our waters. In a warm summer it is sometimes in shoals of enormous numbers. It looks like a pale blue or green bell, with tentacles hanging from its centre, and is completely harmless. Look out for the possibility that leatherback turtles are preying on them.

Length 15cm

PORTUGUESE MAN-O-WAR *Physalia physalis*
An exotic visitor which looks a bit like a child's balloon, the man-o-war is pale blue, with a crenellated crest of a pinkish colour. It can be difficult to convince anyone that it is an animal and not man-made. From the float hangs a complicated cluster of stinging cells in long tentacles. The Portuguese man-o-war enjoys life in

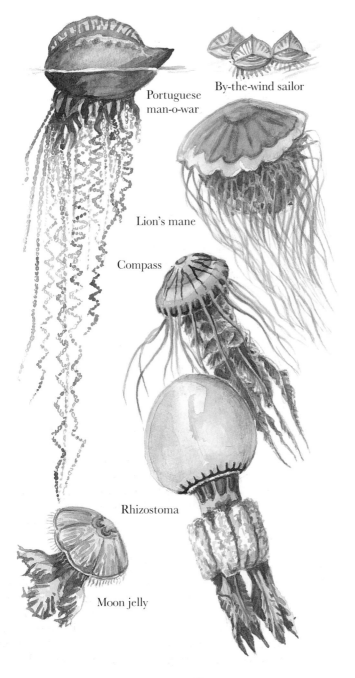

Portuguese
man-o-war

By-the-wind sailor

Lion's mane

Compass

Rhizostoma

Moon jelly

warmer latitudes, floating with the Gulf Stream, but the North Atlantic current and strong south-westerlies may bring it to the coasts of southwest Ireland, Devon and Cornwall, sometimes in large numbers. The air-filled bladder acts as a sail so that the jellyfish is driven by winds as well as currents. Its long tentacles sting and paralyse fish to provide its nourishment and cause painful swellings in humans, which may last several hours. Correct procedure is to apply ammonia and relax!

Diameter 10cm

BY-THE-WIND SAILOR (Jack by-the-wind)
Velella velella

A thin, half-disc sail drives this jellyfish, tentacles trailing. The sail is set at an angle to the 'hull', and the young jellyfish is born to sail either on the port or the starboard tack, so that at least half of them won't end up on the nearest beach.

'In the late summer of some years, along the shores of Devon and Cornwall, or those of southern Ireland, we may find washed up by the waves, large numbers of little objects which at first sight look more like manufactured toys of plastic than things of nature. Oblong in shape, each is like a miniature raft measuring up to 2½ inches long by 1½ inches broad; it has a triangular fin set like a sail diagonally across it. Indeed that is just what the fin is: a sail set to catch the wind, and drive the animal along the surface of the sea like a small model of a sailing barge. "Jack sail-by-the-wind", the old sailors used to call them; today I do not suppose the steamship men, travelling fast, ever notice them ...'

Sir Alister Hardy, *The World of Plankton*,
Collins New Naturalist, 1956

CTENOPHORES

SEA GOOSEBERRY
Pleurobrachia pileus

*Length of tentacles
140mm*

A tiny gelatinous ball, about the size of an edible gooseberry, the sea gooseberry floats below the surface in immense numbers in the summer; it is best seen in front of your mask while snorkelling. With their sticky tentacles, they shimmer as they swim in pursuit of even smaller plankton.

COMB JELLY *Beroe cucumis*

*Length
150mm*

Sometimes seen in large numbers swimming about at the surface, these ctenophores look like near-transparent vegetable marrows. Eight rows of beating plates drive this delicate lavender animal, which has no tentacles but a large mouth which opens wide to engulf lesser plankton such as sea gooseberries. Comb jellies will also be staring you in the face when you snorkel in British waters.

CRUSTACEANS

GOOSE BARNACLE *Lepas anatifera*

It is always worth examining a floating branch or plank, for a long-travelled piece of wood will often carry passengers. During time at sea the surface of floating timber may become colonised by creatures which, floating about in the plankton, are looking for a more permanent home for the next stage of their development. Acorn barnacles and goose barnacles are most likely to be found on the outside surfaces. The goose barnacles, curious creatures with a striking likeness to the head and neck of a bird, are stalked creatures that cement themselves to the wood in warmer parts of the Atlantic. In the days of slow-moving ships they attached themselves in vast numbers below the waterline and then grew fat, doing no good to the vessel's hydrodynamic shape and much reducing her speed.

Like the more familiar acorn barnacles on the shore, the goose barnacle opens protective plates to reveal feathery cirri, which filter food from passing plankton. Originating from more southerly latitudes, these beautiful creatures are usually destined to die on our beaches, but at sea they can be found feeding in all their feathery glory.

MOLLUSCS
(sea-going snails)

VIOLET SEA SNAIL (Bubble-raft snail)
Janthina janthina

A sea-going snail which is suspended under a raft of foamy bubbles, which it blows continuously, the violet sea snail preys on jellyfish like the by-the-wind sailor and the Portuguese man-o-war. It lives in the open ocean but is sometimes carried to our waters and beaches by inconvenient currents.

SHIPWORM *Teredo navalis*

The outside of drifting timber may be colonised by barnacles, but there are very likely to be other creatures active inside. Since the earliest days of civilisation ships have suffered from attacks of 'worm'.

The shipworm is not a worm at all, though it certainly looks like one. It is in fact a particularly destructive bivalve snail. It may be as much as 30cm long, but at the end of its body is a shell, greatly reduced in size and functioning as a highly specialised boring device. It penetrates timber in its larval stage, making a very small entrance hole. Once inside it takes a smart right-angle turn and digs out a tunnel parallel to the surface, cutting its tunnel as it grows with a twisting movement of its shell and literally eating away at the plank, out of sight of unwary sailors. There are three species in British waters, the largest being *Teredo norvegicus*, which is also the commonest (tropical

The shipworm leaves a calcareous deposit which forms the tube that is all that can normally be seen of this creature.

species may grow to a metre and a half!). It may be revealed by splitting the timber open, although the presence of many small, round, cleanly cut holes is also a clue.

Fouling by barnacles and seaweed reduced the speed of a ship and was dealt with by regular careening and scraping, but until the underwater sheathing of timber hulls with copper no one could counter the destructive marine borers. It was found that the interaction of sea water with the copper produced a slow release of copper salt solution which was toxic to the shipworm. Copper is expensive, so today the work of discouraging attack by marine borers is done by anti-fouling paints that often use the same principle of slowly releasing a toxic copper solution.

FISH

SUNFISH
Mola mola

The sunfish is a large fish from tropical waters which drifts with ocean currents in the same way as jellyfish and plankton. In summer it sometimes appears off the southwestern shores of the British Isles. It is the tip of its dorsal fin showing above water that earns the sunfish its name, for it seems to bask in the sun. The fin may be mistaken for a shark's but is quite a different shape. It may also lie on its side at the surface.

Length to 3m

A close relative, the truncated sunfish, *Ranzania laevis*, may occur off the British coast, again in the summer.

BASKING SHARK
Cetorhinus maximus

*Length
to 12m in
British waters*

*Weight
to 7 tonnes*

The harmless and magnificent basking shark is almost the largest fish in the world, second only to the tropical whale shark. Nobody knows where basking sharks spend the winter, but they appear off the southwestern coast of Britain in May or June and move slowly north, until they may be seen off Norway in August. Sometimes alone, sometimes with a few others, and sometimes in parties of anything up to a hundred, the basking shark cruises inshore, swimming sluggishly along, with its blunt snout, dorsal fin and the upper part of its tail fin breaking the surface. It gets its name from the habit of lying motionless on the surface, enjoying the warmth of the sun, but in deep water it has been known to leap clear in a spectacular breach.

Huge though it is, the basking shark feeds entirely on plankton, mainly copepods. It swims with its mouth open, drawing in vast quantities of water which passes through its gills. The plankton is filtered by a sieve-like structure formed by interlocking gill rakes, like the teeth of a comb. At a speed of two knots it is said to sieve the seafood from 2,000 cubic metres of seawater every hour – the equivalent of an Olympic-size swimming pool. It has no swim-bladder and gains buoyancy from its massive liver, which represents a quarter of its weight.

The basking shark's indifference to people is remarkable, so it was easily harpooned for its liver by inshore fishermen in small-scale commercial fisheries, which enjoyed moderate success in past years. Its liver was formerly in demand for the oil fisheries on the coasts of Scotland and Ireland. One liver yielded about 125 gallons. In Ireland, one of its uses was as a dressing for the bull skins which clad curraghs, boats with lightly built frames covered with hides.

Divers may swim close to a cruising shark and the only real danger is that a startled or injured fish may damage man or boat by a lash of its powerful tail. If you must go close, approach slowly and from astern, but do not harass them. They are protected from capture or disturbance in British waters under the Wildlife and Countryside Act (1981). Protection is also currently proposed under the Convention on International Trade in Endangered Species (CITES).

TO REPORT BASKING SHARK SIGHTINGS

Contact the Marine Conservation Society (9 Gloucester Road, Ross-on-Wye, Herefordshire HR9 5BU; tel: 01989 566017; web: www.mcsuk.org/baskingshark.html) which offers report cards for recording basking shark sightings.

To report strandings and entanglements, telephone Seaquest in England (01392 279244), the strandings co-ordinator at the Scottish Agricultural College in Scotland (01463 243030), or the strandings co-ordinator in Wales (01348 87500).

TURTLES

'What other bodily being possesses such a citadel wherein to resist the assaults of Time?' Herman Melville, 'The Encantadas', 1854

Turtles are marine tortoises, their limbs modified into paddles. Unlike tortoises, their heads do not retract into their shells. They come ashore only to deposit and bury their eggs above the tideline of a tropical beach, to be incubated by the warmth of the sun. A number of species have been recorded in British and Irish waters, but the most likely visitor is the leatherback turtle, which is better able to survive in northern waters. Other species are very difficult to identify at sea, or even when stranded ashore.

Three other turtles, carried from Caribbean and Floridian waters, and not so happy in the cold North Atlantic, have also been recorded in our area:

COMMON LOGGERHEAD
Caretta caretta
Carapace 1m, almost 2m overall

KEMP'S RIDLEY
Lepidochelys kempii
Carapace 70cm

HAWKSBILL
Eretmochelys imbricata
Carapace less than 1m

LEATHERBACK TURTLE
(Leathery, luth)
Dermochelys coriacea

The most common visitor to our coasts, and the easiest to identify, quite apart from its huge size by comparison with the others, is the leatherback turtle. Its carapace is covered by an oily skin which is inhospitable to the barnacles that one might otherwise expect to see on its back. It is easily recognised by the fore-and-aft keels which run along its back. Mostly they are seen at sea from summer to early winter. They feed on jellyfish. Once, when sailing off the south Cornish coast, on a flat calm day, we came across a leatherback which was biting into a large specimen of *Rhizostoma*. It bit and tore with such gusto that the jellyfish span like a top.

*Carapace
2m
overall length
to 3m*

*Weight
to 350kg*

BIRDS

A bird's secret weapon is its feathers, the development of which allowed these creatures to spread and thrive all over the planet. Feathers not only keep birds warm and provide opportunities for colourful display, they give the power to fly economically, to escape from enemies and to explore food and breeding opportunities wherever they may be. But feathers are subject to wear and tear, and to the ageing effects of the ultra-violet rays in sunlight, so there has to be a continual programme of maintenance and periodic replacement. You may often see birds scratching their heads in flight, or indulging in hair-raising, preening acrobatics when they are alone, or sometimes while they glide downwind, but generally speaking they choose the time and the place for their seasonal moults with care.

Wing shapes vary enormously, but many ocean-going seabirds, such as fulmars and albatrosses, have long and narrow wings. They are gliders, made for effortless soaring, making use of thermals or the lift from wave-winds. Shearwaters have long narrow wings, too, but they are more flexible than those of albatrosses, and they are able to 'fly' underwater to a certain extent. Auks have short, narrow wings and fly through the air with difficulty, but they manoeuvre underwater with great skill. Great auks were master submariners, with even shorter wings, but they could not fly at all and suffered extinction as a direct result.

Typically, seabirds have webbed feet, though in the case of the phalaropes these are almost non-existent. Storm-petrels walk on the sea with them; cormorants use them as propulsion units in diving and active pursuit of prey. In many species they are useful not only in assisting water-borne take-offs but also as brakes and control surfaces in seemingly difficult aerial manoeuvres.

Classic experiments have confirmed that seabirds are well able to find their way about the unmarked oceans. When Ronald Lockley had Manx shearwaters flown by aeroplane to Rio de Janeiro in an early experiment in 1937, they returned to their nest-burrow on Skokholm Island off the coast of Wales in just 16 days, averaging 460 miles (740km) per day.

In coasting along inshore waters, seabirds use the visual signals of cliffs, headlands, 'conspic houses' and doubtless lighthouses too, just as sailors do. And in making journeys out of sight of land, they navigate just as seamen do, by observing heavenly bodies and measuring time using their highly efficient biological clocks. They are perfectly capable of setting a course and measuring distance covered. They use a variety of senses in gathering information. The sounds of waves, distant echoes from far-off cliffs and mountains, even smell in the case of tubenosed species. And with magnetite in their nervous system they are able to sense the Earth's magnetic field, so even have an inbuilt compass; in a magnetic storm they become disoriented, exactly as one would expect.

So birds have access to a whole range of navigational aids and make use of them according to the weather conditions and problems they face at any particular time. Little is known about these aids, but what is certain is that they work extremely well, except on those occasions when foul weather deprives them of stimulus.

Seabirds benefited greatly from the protection begun in 1869 when the Sea Birds Protection Bill outlawed egg-collecting and shooting for sport.

EXPLOITATION OF COASTAL BIRDS

*Barnacle goose,
F W Frohawk, 1905*

*'Barnacles breed
unnaturally by
corruption and taste
very unsavoury. Poor
men eat them, rich
men hate them, and
wise men reject
them when they
have other meat.'
Thomas Moffatt,
'Health's
Improvement',
1655*

BRANTA LEUCOPSIS

Various species of coastal birds have been harvested with enthusiasm, either as eggs, as chicks or as adults, for any number of uses.

From the plentiful supply of bones in prehistoric middens, we can say with some certainty that early man not only ate gamebirds but that he sampled waterfowl and seabirds. Fossil bones in caves have shown that Stone Age hunters ate auks as well as gannets and geese. But the barnacle goose has perhaps the most curious claim to fame. In early times, no one knew where they bred; their arrival every autumn was regarded as something of a mystery, explained only by a bizarre link with a marine crustacean – the goose barnacle, *Lepas anatifera* (see page 16). The geese arrived in their Irish and Scottish grounds at about the time of the September gales, coinciding with the large-scale strandings of barnacles, thrown ashore attached to floating branches or driftwood. (Goose barnacles bear a striking resemblance to the neck and beak of a bird, complete with 'feathers' in the shape of their filter mechanisms, the cirri.)

The popular myth emerged that no egg or nest was involved in the development of the bird, but that the infant stage of the barnacle geese was generated spontaneously and nourished by trees. At a time when dietary laws were more closely followed by the religious, the advantage of believing in the maritime origin of the fat bird was obvious; coming from the sea, the barnacle goose could safely be classified as a fish, suitable for the table on a Friday:

> 'Bishops and religious men in some parts of Ireland do not scruple to dine off these birds at a time of fasting because they are not flesh nor born of flesh.'
>
> Giraldus Cambrensis, 1185

This myth flourished till Pope Innocent III forbade the practice by decree in the 12th century, but it lingered for several centuries more in the remoter parts of Ireland. To this day, the annual gatherings of breeding seabirds provide remote islanders with a welcome addition to the larder. But islanders have always been forced by circumstances to take greater care of their precious food resources than profligate mainlanders, who have over-exploited wild stocks without regard to the long-term consequences. Farmed sensibly, coastal colonies of seabirds offer a useful source of good food, and the prudent farmer has the long-term health and interest of his charges at heart.

'Certain trees bear fruit which, decaying within, produces a worm which, as it subsequently developes, becomes hairy and feathered, and, provided wings, flies like a bird.'
John Gerard,
'Generall Historie Of Plantes', 1597

> 'So rotten sides of broken shippes do change to Barnacles;
> O, Transformation strange!
> 'Twas first a greene Tree; then a gallant Hull,
> Lately a mushroom, now a flying Gull.'
>
> Guillaume de Saluste, 1578

Puffin. From Willughby's 'Ornithology', 1678

'*They [puffins] are plucked, split open like kippers, cured and hung up to dry on strings stretched across the cottages; and whenever a native feels hungry he simply pulls one down from the line, flings it on the fire to grill, and forthwith has his lunch without the aid of knife, fork, plate or napkin.*' Richard Kearton, 'With Nature and a Camera', 1899

Remote islanders have always taken good care to husband their stock in the interest of future survival. Although a tithe of the newly arrived adult birds was taken in spring, plus a proportion of the first laying of eggs, they made sure that enough birds were left with at least one full clutch, and only a sustainable proportion of young were taken. It was on islands that Neolithic man learnt the benefits of seasonal occupation, taking seabird eggs and chicks while their sheep and cattle grazed the rich summer pasture.

Seabird eggs have always been enthusiastically harvested. In times of hardship, such as during war, the eggs of gulls have made a useful addition to the national larder. In years past, the eggs of several species of gulls were taken in vast quantities. Black-headed gull colonies were conveniently established among accessible sand dunes and islands on lakes. Their nests were worked systematically at the beginning of the season and the harvesting called off before the gulls became too discouraged to complete their clutches. As late as 1935, Leadenhall Market in London traded 300,000 black-headed gull eggs a year.

Gulls offered the convenience of habitually breeding in large numbers in places more easily accessible than the cliff-laying auks. Quite apart from that, they also lay a larger clutch, usually of three or four eggs, and, as with the domestic hen, they will continue laying when the eggs are taken from them. If the colonies are farmed intelligently, they are capable of supplying a sustained yield of great value. At Ravenglass, in Cumbria, for example, some 15,000 pairs of black-headed gulls nest on the sand dunes. In the mid-19th century, similar gulleries were encouraged by the construction of suitable nesting islands; one of the annual activities was the spring harvesting of gulls and their eggs. It is said that the gulls were grain-fed to make them more palatable.

Egg-collecting on coastal cliffs was a great deal more difficult, but 130,000 guillemot eggs were taken from the cliffs on the Yorkshire coast at Bempton in 1884. Puffins, as well as other auks, were much treasured and taken in enormous numbers. In the 1870s, for instance, something like 100,000 were killed for their feathers and meat and marketed in London, along with fat shearwaters, as 'puffling'.

Seabird populations are remarkably resilient in the face of natural predators, but the golden goose is a finite resource. Exploitation of mainland colonies developed on altogether too greedy a scale. The increase in human population and the more widespread availability of firearms, coupled with vastly improved means of transport, reduced accessible seabird populations markedly. From about 1830, the boatmen of Bridlington and Scarborough became involved in a disreputable trade which devastated the Flamborough Head colonies. Chartered by parties of a few dozen 'gentlemen' at a time, pleasure steamers took so-called sportsmen to the foot of the cliffs, from where they could indulge in target practice with shotguns. The result was a systematic destruction of the sitting auks and gulls. A contemporary correspondent (quoted in *British Birds* by F O Morris, 1850) wrote of two boats 'literally laden with birds, the boatmen sitting on them, and the birds heaped up in the bow and the stern above the gunwale'. This kind of mindless

'The exercise they affect most is climbing of steep rocks. He is the prettiest man who ventures upon the most inaccessible, though all they gain is the eggs of the fowles, and the honour to dye, as many of their ancestors, by breaking of their necks.'
Sir George Mackenzie of Tarbat, 1675

Adult puffins were caught at St Kilda and are still caught in Iceland by the use of a 'flegg-net', a sort of man-sized butterfly net. 19th-century engraving

slaughter also went on at other seabird sites, such as Bass Rock near Edinburgh, the Isle of May off the coast of Fife, and the islands of the Pembrokeshire coast, but it was in the Yorkshire vicarage of Bridlington that dissenting opinion found its voice and an association for the protection of birds was formed. Clergymen sent a letter to *The Times* newspaper, public opinion was stirred, and the first of many Sea Bird Acts was passed in 1869.

This was only the beginning of effective legal protection, and in any case birds were not only taken for their meat and eggs. In the latter part of the 19th century, kittiwakes were massacred mercilessly on the

A delicately spread corpse decorated the 'Diaz chapeau' on the title page of 'Myra's Journal', April 1882

Bristol Channel island of Lundy by fishermen who collected the wings of juvenile birds and sent them to London for the fashion trade. This was at a time when it was regarded as the height of fashion to decorate hats and gowns with the plumage of dead birds.

> 'At Clovelly, opposite Lundy Island, there was a regular staff for preparing the plumes; and fishing smacks, with extra boats and crews, used to commence their work of destruction by daybreak on the 1st of August (when the close time under the Seabirds Preservation Act expired), continuing this proceeding for upwards of a fortnight. In many cases the wings were torn off the wounded birds before they were dead, the mangled victims being tossed back into the water. On one day 700 birds were sent back to Clovelly, on another 500, and so on; and, allowing for starved nestlings, it is well within the mark to say that at least 9000 of these inoffensive birds were destroyed during the fortnight.'
>
> William Yarrell, *A History of British Birds*, 1885

It was on St Kilda, the most remote of the Outer Hebridean Islands, that the exploitation of natural seabird resources was carried out with the greatest care and skill. The welfare of the island's human community relied on successful harvesting for at least 14 centuries. A population of a hundred people sustained themselves at a level above mere subsistence, and with a degree of happiness. Islanders learnt, the hard way, that it was safe to take more than half of the eggs laid by guillemots at first laying, because, provided the season was young enough, the females would lay again to replace their single egg. The auks were then left undisturbed. Each year they took some two thousand of both the adult gannets and the fat chicks – the gugas – providing meat, oil for lamps, feathers for beds and pillows and skins for carpet slippers. The birds were taken either by nooses extended on poles or were simply clubbed on the head and thrown into the sea to be collected by boats waiting below. A high degree of courage was required, both in the cliff-climbing and in the seamanship, to say nothing of the danger of being hit on the head by a dead guga weighing ten pounds (4.5kg). The islanders took their tithe of fat young fulmars and gannets just before they flew the nest, much later in the summer. Acting as prudent predators, they left the breeding hordes no worse off than when they came.

In addition to the gannet catch, the islanders collected an average of 12,000 fulmars each year, a half of the island's production. Fulmars have been taken in enormous numbers from the seabird cliffs of Norway and Iceland, but, until the late 19th century, the remote island community of St Kilda was the only British outpost where they bred. As Thomas Pennant wrote of St Kilda in 1776: 'no bird is of such use to the islanders as this: the fulmar supplies them with oil for their lamps, down for their beds, a delicacy for their wounds and a medicine for their distempers.'

Though the carnage may seem appalling to our 21st-century sensibilities, this island community lived in natural harmony with the seabirds on their doorstep. Their lives were lived only by virtue of the existence of the seabirds, but by all accounts they were satisfying lives, both culturally and physically. The Hebridean island of Sula Sgeir hosts the only British gannetry from which young gugas may still be taken. The men of Lewis have the legal right to harvest there. If the cull is of young gannets, the effect on breeding numbers is small, but the taking of adults does have an adverse effect unless there is a steady recruitment of breeding stock from other gannetries. With the species doing well at the moment, there is no shortage of willing recruits.

Changing attitudes to exploitation allowed gannets to show a steady increase in population during the 20th century. Currently there is said to be a total population of some 150,000 breeding pairs in Britain and Ireland, but they are almost entirely confined to remote islands where they are relatively free from human interference. Mainland colonies of seabirds have been ruthlessly over-exploited by men who have not had the long-term interests of their prey at heart, and birds have suffered accordingly.

Despite that, our coast continues to host one of the richest concentrations of seabirds in the world.

'Multitudes of the inhabitants of each cluster of islands feed, during the season, on the eggs of the birds of the cliffs. The method of taking them is so very hazardous, as to satisfy one of the extremity to which the poor people are driven for want of food. The dauntless fowlers ascend, pass intrepidly from one cliff-face to the other, collect the birds and eggs and descend with the same indifference.'
Thomas Pennant, 'Arctic Zoology', 1784

DIVERS

Divers are superb swimmers and underwater hunters. They come ashore only to nest. On land they are somewhat clumsy, since their legs are set well back on their bodies to be used as propulsion units in the water. They swim low in the water, submerging smoothly down in search of prey. In flight they have narrow, pointed wings and they droop fore-and-aft, unlike the cormorant which holds its head high.

RED-THROATED DIVER
Gavia stellata

Length
50–60cm

Wingspan
106–116cm

The smallest of the divers, red-throated divers have an uptilted bill and legs set well back on their bodies. During breeding, their grey necks sport a red-brick throat patch which is more easily seen in paintings than in real life!

A hardy species, originating in the Arctic as high as 80° north, these birds come ashore only for breeding, arriving at their breeding areas in late April/early May, sometimes alone and sometimes in small colonies, choosing the borders of sheltered marine and freshwater lochs in hilly country in the north and west of Scotland and northern Ireland. In June they frequent freshwater pools, and sometimes large lakes, with a profusion of bankside vegetation. The nest is a flattened patch of greenery or sometimes a mossy, weedy heap, very close to shallow water so that the birds can slide in and out with ease. The clutch is usually of two eggs, incubated by both parents for 24–29 days. At this stage they are vulnerable to disturbance. If all goes well the newly hatched chicks leave the nest on their second day, already able to swim, and are cared for by both parents, typically riding on their backs. The adult birds commute to inshore tidal waters to hunt for food, pursuing small fish which are caught underwater by grabbing, not

spearing. Fledging is in 43 days, when the young are independent and go to sea; they reach maturity at the age of two or three years.

In winter, red-throated divers are relatively common in small flocks off the coast, especially in the east. By this time of year they have lost their red throats and their heads become almost all white. During this time they are the palest of all the divers.

DIVER CALLS

On the water the red-throated diver calls an assortment of croaks and wailing noises, while in flight it tends to employ a duck-like quacking, 'kwuk-kwuk-kwuk'. In Shetland it is known as the 'rain goose' as it is alleged to become more vocal before the heavens debouch, although there is precious little evidence to support this claim.

DIVING BIRDS IN WINTER PLUMAGE

Red-throated
diver

Black-throated
diver

Great northern
diver

White-billed
diver

Great-crested
grebe

Red-necked
grebe

Slavonian
grebe

Black-necked
grebe

Little grebe

TUBENOSES

Petrels and shearwaters form part of the 'tubenose' order, which also includes the albatrosses. Their grooved and horny-plated bills are hooked for catching fish. They are of medium size, 38–64cm long, with streamlined bodies and long, narrow, pointed wings. In terms of colouring they are fairly drab birds, dark above and whitish below. Adapted for an ocean-going life, they swim well, having webbed feet placed well back on the body to act as powerful paddles in water, but these serve only to help them shuffle clumsily on land, stumbling around their breeding ledges or underground burrows.

The long narrow wings of shearwaters allow for a flight pattern which involves a burst of fast wing-beats followed by a spell of high-speed gliding low over the waves, tipping from side to side, first showing the underside and then upperparts as they seem to 'shear' the surface. Fulmars have stubbier bodies, flying alternately with a burst of flapping and then stiff gliding. Apart from fulmars, tubenoses do not follow ships routinely though they may sometimes keep station for a while.

In most tubenoses, except the albatrosses, the 'tube' is on top of the upper mandible, with the opening half way along. Its primary function is to filter salt out of sea water.

FULMAR
Fulmarus glacialis

The name 'fulmar' comes from the Norse and literally means 'foul gull', after its musty smell and its habit of spitting noisome stomach oil at aggressors. Fulmars are superficially gull-like but stockier and bull-necked, with a stubby, tubenose bill and, at close range, a dark eye. In flight they behave like a small albatross ('mollymawk' is a common name which became transferred to the albatrosses of the Southern Ocean), interspersing flapping with stiff-winged gliding, the leading edge of the wing straight, as opposed to the bow-shape of gulls' wings. They have grey upperparts with pale-blue wrist-patches. Highly gregarious birds, they may congregate on the surface of the sea in their thousands.

The fulmar is a prime example of a polymorphic

Length
45–50cm

Wingspan
102–112cm

species, in which two distinct forms exist in one interbreeding population (see also *Skuas*). The variation is genetically based and not a distinction based on sex. In the case of the fulmar, the proportion of the darker, so-called 'blue phase' individuals increases with latitude further north. As is the case with skuas, these polymorphic species are characteristic of northern waters, for reasons which remain unexplained – there is no evidence that there is any advantage one way or the other in terms of breeding success, as birds representing one morph will happily mate with birds from the other.

Fulmar drawn by Friderich Martens, who visited St Kilda in 1697. 'This isle abounds with an infinite number of fowl …'

In courtship fulmars indulge in water-dances, raucous displays by as many as a dozen birds on the water close to the nesting cliffs. At the nest site itself – a mere scrape in the turf or soil of a convenient ledge – they also tend to garrulous cackling. They breed colonially on the greener parts of coastal cliffs where there is easy access to open seas. Like all petrels, they lay a single white egg, usually in mid-May, incubating for about 50 days. After the long period of feeding, the chick is abandoned to make its first solo flight unaided (fledglings are likely to be on their nest ledges till early September). The young birds then disperse to live at sea for several years before returning to their birthplace to prospect for a nest-site.

Adults range far over the Barents Sea and the North Atlantic, but have a strong attachment to their nest-place, often visiting it outside the breeding season. The breeding pair remain faithful to one another.

Fulmars have given us a most remarkable example of range expansion in recent times. Until the 1870s the only British breeding station was on the remote island of St Kilda, where 20,000 pairs bred and they were a valued resource, the annual harvest numbering some 12,000.

It seems likely that it was the Icelandic population which provided the impetus for fulmars to extend their range south to the British Isles by way of the Faeroes. There is still controversy about the reasons for their explosive extension of range, but the 20th-century increase in trawling and whaling activities certainly provided fuel; their natural food is plankton and small fish, but they took enthusiastically to following whalers for offal. In 1847, the naturalist Thomas Bewick described them thus:

'These birds are extremely greedy and gluttonous, and will devour any floating putrid substances, such as the filth from the ships, which they fearlessly follow. They also pursue the whales, but particularly the bloody track of those that are wounded, and in such great flocks as thereby sometimes to discover the prize to the fishers, with whom they generally share; for when the huge animal is no longer able to sink, the Fulmars, in multitudes, alight upon it, and ravenously pluck off and devour lumps of the blubber, till they can hold no more.'

Sometimes fulmars will follow ships in large flocks. In the whaling days, they gathered at the carcasses, tearing blubber till they were replete. More recently they have followed Atlantic and North Sea trawlers to gorge on the offal and by-catch thrown over the side. Fuelled by this sort of food availability, they increased and colonised ever further south, though the warming of the northeast Atlantic may also have been a contributory factor. By the 1970s almost all suitable cliffs around Britain, Ireland and the coast of Brittany in France had been settled.

Fulmars also live long lives, possibly up to a hundred years. The oldest recovery of a British-ringed bird was in Orkney: a fulmar over 51 years old.

Fulmar. Engraving by Thomas Bewick, 'A History of British Birds', Newcastle, 1847

MANX SHEARWATER
Puffinus puffinus

Mediterranean
shearwater

*Length
30–38cm*

*Wingspan
76–82cm*

The most common shearwaters in the northeast
Atlantic, these drab 'soot and whitewash' seabirds
are dark above and whitish below. They are of medium
size, with streamlined bodies and long, narrow, pointed
wings which allow for a flight pattern that involves a
burst of fast wing-beats followed by a spell of high-
speed gliding low over the waves, tipping from side to
side, first showing the underside then the upperparts
and seeming to 'shear' the surface. Unlike fulmars they
do not follow ships routinely, though they may sometimes
keep station for a while. Grooved and horny-plated
bills are hooked for fish-catching. Adapted for an ocean-
going life, they swim well, having webbed feet placed
well back on the body, acting as powerful paddles in

water, but serving only to shuffle clumsily on land, when they stumble into their underground burrows.

After wintering in the South Atlantic off the South American coast, Manx shearwaters migrate to the island colonies off the Scottish and Welsh coasts in April. At this time of year, and well into summer, they congregate in their tens of thousands in 'rafts' on the surface of the sea, socialising and waiting for the light to fade before they pluck up enough courage to run the gull gauntlet and come ashore to their nesting sites (they do this under cover of darkness in order to reduce the hazard of predatory gulls; in the same way, underground breeding also serves to protect both chicks and adults from the gulls which so persistently harass them). At last light on a calm day, the spectacle of thousands of auks and shearwaters on the sea and swirling around the cliffs is something to savour.

On the Hebridean island of Rum, Manx shearwaters breed high up on a mountainside, a couple of thousand feet above sea level. At the more typical, and accessible, site on Skomer Island off Pembrokeshire their burrows, and their nocturnal activity, seem to permeate the whole of island life in the late spring.

Here, as elsewhere, a single white egg is laid about a metre from the entrance, then incubated by both parents in turn for over 50 days. During the fledging period the adults take it in turn to fly several hundred miles to the Bay of Biscay to collect sardines with which to feed their chick. In diving for sardines they swim like penguins, using their wings for propulsion to reach depths of up to 20m. Fledging takes 70 days, at which point the chick is abandoned to find its own way out of the safety of the burrow, to launch itself from the cliff top, and to fish for itself. It reaches sexual maturity after about five years.

Manx shearwaters are great travellers, making remarkable journeys of many thousands of miles from their breeding islands to their wintering quarters in the waters off the coasts of Brazil and Argentina. They live long lives. An individual ringed on the island of Bardsey in the 1950s is still going strong having clocked some five million miles.

There may be something like a quarter of a million pairs of 'Manxies' breeding in the British Isles; on Skomer Island alone there are over 160,000.

The Mediteranean shearwater, P. yelkouan, is duller than the Manx, and with dusky underparts; it is sometimes seen in British waters. More unusual shearwaters, as illustrated on page 159, may also be seen in these waters in autumn.

STORM-PETRELS

Storm-petrels are wholeheartedly marine. Of all flying birds they are the most successfully adapted to sea-going life. The smallest of all seabirds, they are little larger than swallows, and indeed share some of their dashing and fluttering flight patterns. They tend to be dark above with pale wing coverts, very often with white rumps and forked tails. Their underparts vary, but are often white. They have deeply grooved, hooked bills which are small and black. Their nostrils are long and tubular; they also have a strong sense of smell, an unusual facility in birds.

Storm-petrels share some characteristics with penguins, to which they are closely related. They are web-footed and are almost helpless on land, shuffling to their nest-burrow aided by their outstretched wings. The northern forms tend to be long-winged and often fork-tailed, whereas the southerners have longer legs and shorter, broader wings.

BRITISH STORM-PETREL
Hydrobates pelagicus

*Length
14–17cm*

*Wingspan
36–39cm*

Sooty-black with a white rump, the storm-petrel is like a sea-going house martin. Unusually for seabirds, storm-petrels have extraordinarily long legs in proportion to their tiny size, and they flutter about, long legs dangling and feet pattering over the waves, looking for all the world as though they were walking on water. So 'ocean-going water-walker' is a splendid scientific name for this charismatic little bird.

Possibly the word 'petrel' comes from the 'pitter-patter' of their feet during wave-walking. More likely is that 'petrel' is a form of 'little Peter', which suggests a biblical connotation of walking on water. The prefix 'storm' probably comes from the birds' association in the minds of mariners, who say their appearance round a ship foretells an imminent blow, or possibly

because the ship's passage provides something of a lee. Or it may be a name bestowed by landsmen who only see the species when, as sometimes happens, the birds are blown ashore in great numbers by a storm at sea. Yet another seamen's name is 'Mother Carey's chickens'. Mother Carey may have been something of a sea-witch whose 'chickens' attended ships in distress in order to report drownings. Prayer might save a good man, but bad sorts were transformed by Mother Carey into stormy petrels, doomed to travel the trackless wastes for ever. Or perhaps Mother Carey was Mater Cara, the Mother Beloved or Virgin Mary, whose chickens kept watch over the faithful.

The British storm-petrel is the smallest seabird in these northwest Atlantic waters. It habitually follows ships at sea, to take advantage of the plankton forced to the surface in their wake, though this makes it vulnerable to the attentions of predators like the peregrine, which has often been seen bringing a 'stormy' to a convenient high point in the rigging, where it is plucked and eaten.

Leach's storm-petrel

Wilson's storm-petrel

In feeding, storm-petrels catch plankton at the surface, picking it off while they hover or walk just at sea level. They tend to feed alone, or in small, loosely knit flocks, but if food is plentiful they may gather in huge numbers. They will crowd enthusiastically around galley waste, sucking oily drops from the water, or tearing fat from a dead whale. Their curiously shaped nostrils give them the ability to smell food at a great distance and they will gather downwind of a whale in order to feed on the oily emulsion of its blow.

Storm-petrels venture ashore only to breed, and, like Manx shearwaters, they take care to arrive and depart during the hours of darkness to avoid predators. They breed sociably, in underground crevices and burrows, or sometimes in drystone walls or ruins, and usually on islands. Typically they exude a musky smell which may reveal the nest burrow, but they also have a characteristic purring call at dusk and during the night. A single egg is laid in June, incubated by both parents in turn for the best part of six weeks. The chick is fed mostly stomach-oil, and flies when it's about two months old.

OIL SECRETION AND EXCRETION

In addition to having large tail glands which yield oil for preening, all members of the petrel family, from the mighty albatross to the sparrow-sized storm-petrel, regurgitate stomach oil through mouth and nostrils. The function of this discharge, which occurs when the bird is alarmed, or stimulated in some way (such as by the appearance of a predator), or in preening and chick-feeding, is somewhat puzzling. In composition it resembles the preen gland oil, and the spermaceti oil of whales. It is rich in vitamins A and D and turns to wax when cold. It appears to be a by-product of the petrel's oil-rich fish and crustacean diet, accumulated after the digestion of the more soluble protein component. The oil is stored in the stomach cells. It has an strong, unpleasantly musky odour which clings persistently to the petrel and its nesting place (and to human flesh and clothes when an observer handles any petrel). In fulmars, including the giant petrel of the southern oceans (appropriately named 'stinker'), the evil-smelling fluid may shoot several feet towards an intruder. Despite its powerful smell, it is perfectly digestible by humans, and is used in the preparation of food by Polynesian and other peoples.

GANNETS & CORMORANTS

Gannets are members of the Sulidae family, while cormorants and shags are members of the Phalacrocoracidae order, but both belong to the pelican order Pelecaniformes, which includes tropicbirds and boobies. All are fish-eating birds, with paddle feet, and all tend to be gregarious and noisy in the colony, but silent at sea.

Only one species of gannet is found around the British Isles. The northern gannet is our largest seabird, about the size of a goose, and is characterised by its feeding behaviour, which involves diving from a great height in pursuit of pelagic fish. It is very rarely seen inland.

Cormorants, meanwhile, are medium-to-large birds, with long necks, longish wings, stiff wedge-shaped tails, slender, cylindrical bills with a sharp hook and strong legs, placed well aft to act as a powerful twin-paddle propulsion unit. The plumage is usually black in the adult, with a purple or green metallic sheen, and sometimes with white underparts. Usually there is a bare patch around the face.

These are coastal birds, rarely out of sight of land, and some even frequent inland waters. Goose-like in flight, they are more diver-like in the water, floating almost below the surface. Slow-moving fish and crustaceans are their main food. Eels are also taken in large numbers. Their technique is to duck-dive and then chase underwater. Jackknifing from the surface, they spring a little into the air and dive head first. Their paddle-feet give propulsion, while their wings act as control surfaces. They work mostly in shallow water, but can dive to 15 fathoms if necessary. Most dive sessions last less than a minute.

Worldwide there are some 30 species of cormorant; in the British Isles we are restricted to two, so we are able to ignore the rest and conveniently call one 'the' cormorant and the other 'the' shag.

NORTHERN GANNET
Sula bassana

*Length
86–96cm*

*Wingspan
165–180cm*

The largest and most spectacular of North Atlantic seabirds, the gannet appears 'whiter than white' at a distance and 'pointed at both ends' when close, with conspicuous black wing-tips.

Their bodies are cigar-shaped and they have long, fairly narrow wings, wedge-shaped tails, stout bills and forward-facing eyes. Gannets are plunge-divers, are powerful in flight, and are double-breasted, with air sacs between the skins to absorb impact when they dive from a great height (which can be as much as 30m, but is more usually around 10m) in pursuit of fast pelagic fish like mackerel. First marking their chosen prey from the air, they close their wings to drop vertically into the water. Specially adapted for this activity, with forward vision and slit nostrils, gannets strike the surface with great force, sending up a tremendous splash and continuing their dive underwater

*'Then too was
driven Oslac beloved,
an exile far from
his native land,
over the rolling waves,
over the ganet-bath.'
Beowulf*

using their feet and wings. The catch may be swallowed underwater or it may be brought to the surface. Usually the dive is brief and the buoyant bird rises, takes off, then circles to dive again.

Though you may see them close inshore, especially in stormy weather, gannets usually hunt far out to sea. With their long white wings tipped with black, they are as big as a turkey and are easily recognised. The white plumage, so strikingly conspicuous in a plunge-dive, probably serves to alert other gannets to the fishing potential of a surface shoal.

In courtship, gannets indulge in highly ritualised displays, bowing, 'sky-pointing' and 'mutual fencing' in pursuit of a strong pair-bond, and to proclaim ownership of a nest-site.

Gannets are highly gregarious, breeding on remote islands and undisturbed cliffs of the Gulf of St Lawrence, Newfoundland, Labrador, Iceland, France, and, more recently, Norway, but a large part of the world population of the North Atlantic gannet is based in the British Isles, where there are 18 breeding colonies. Most are stationed on the north and west coasts of Scotland and around Ireland, but they have a historic base on Bass Rock in the Firth of Forth near Edinburgh. There are also sites on the islands of Pembrokeshire in Wales, off the Channel Island of Alderney and on the Yorkshire coast at Bempton.

The bulky nests of seaweed and assorted flotsam are sometimes on level areas at cliff tops, or on the steepest slopes and the most precipitous ledges. The glutinous seaweed sticks tight to the rocks, while the nest cup is elaborately decorated, very often with pieces of brightly coloured rope thrown overboard from fishing boats and left to drift in tidal currents until they end up on beaches, snarled up in small boat propellers or, indeed, as nest adornments. Sadly, these scraps of netting often prove fatal to the gannet chicks, which become entangled in them, and it is not unusual to see an adult or sub-adult gannet flying the oceans with a permanent necklace of long-lasting synthetic rope.

Both parents take turns in caring for a single egg, which is incubated by their webbed feet, placed one over the other, enfolding the egg like a glove. Hatching after six weeks or so, the chick is fed for a further two

Black-browed albatross and young gannet

months by both parents, who regurgitate a rich bouillabaisse of half-digested fish. Then, abandoned, it finds its own way down to the sea to swim about, learn to fish for itself, or perish. Soon it will teach itself to fly and migrate south to spend the winter off the west coast of Africa, travelling without benefit of parental guidance but flying to a pattern programmed into its biological computer. Working to the simplest form of navigation, it will follow a set compass course for a given time, making no allowance for leeway. Doubtless many individuals go astray, but enough survive to learn from the experience and to develop more sophisticated navigational skills.

After wintering in the fish-rich seas of the eastern Atlantic, gannets return home to their birthplace, rather late in the breeding season. Here they merely act as spectators, presumably learning the ropes. As the years go by they travel less extensively and become more attached to their colony, working between the nest area and the fishing-grounds. They are not mature until they are four or five years old, when they reach full adult plumage.

While immature gannets are away at sea during the winter, the adults spend most of their time near their ancestral breeding places. In fact adult gannets are more or less sedentary by comparison with most seabirds; the male birds, especially, tend to stay near their breeding-cliffs or islands, ready to bag the best nest-sites in spring. In deep winter the gannets of the Western Approaches will be adults in their snow-white plumage. These cover many miles on their fishing expeditions, and may hail from the Welsh strongholds off Pembrokeshire, the southern coast of Ireland, the Channel Islands, or the Sept Isles off the coast of Brittany. Unlike boobies, gannets may also roost at sea, congregating in large flotillas.

After a disastrous decline in the 19th century as a result of mindless persecution of mainland colonies, their population enjoyed a general increase in the 20th century. Only one British gannetry, at Sula Sgeir, north of Lewis in the Hebrides, is still legally raided for the fat 'gugas', which were once commonly eaten at Scottish banquets as 'a most delicate fowle'.

CORMORANT

Phalacrocorax carbo

The word 'cormorant' derives from the Latin *'corvus marinus'* or the French *'cor marin'*, but either way the bird is a basically a sea crow. The size of the bird, its colour and its rounded wings all bear a certain resemblance to those of a crow. They are essentially coastal birds, though over the last few decades they have penetrated inland to establish new breeding colonies, especially in the southeast where the continental race, *sinensis*, nests in trees.

Cormorant plumage lacks waterproofing. The contour feathers are modified to allow air out and water in when underwater, an adaptation well suited to diving birds (human divers have to carry weights in order to achieve the desirable negative buoyancy for deep diving). Also, their bones are denser than those of most birds, and less pneumatic, and they have no air

Length
80–100cm

Wingspan
130–160cm

sacs under the skin, characteristics which make gannets, boobies and pelicans so buoyant. They swallow pebbles for ballast and possibly to adjust their trim. Diving birds have a blood system which suits their way of life. The primary oxygen-carrying component is myoglobin rather than the haemoglobin which the human system uses. Myoglobin carries more oxygen molecules, and this increased oxygen capacity allows birds to remain submerged for long periods and dive to great depths. These facilities serve the cormorant well underwater, but after a fishing session it has only a sluggish flight capability and must ventilate its wings to dry them, which accounts for the umbrella-like stance it often adopts while standing on a convenient post drying its wings.

In fact cormorants do not spend a lot of time in the water, unless they are actively feeding. Swimming low, with very little of their topsides showing, they fish by underwater pursuit. Sometimes, backs awash, they slide underwater gently, but more often they take a purposeful leap and jackknife down to search for prey, propelling themselves with the broad-webbed paddles of their feet. Their wings are closed underwater, except for during braking or manoeuvring. Mostly they hunt in shoal water, inside the 10m mark, often over a bottom that may be less than a metre down. They may stay down for a few seconds, half a minute, or sometimes over a minute.

Though they seem to lead idle lives, cormorants work hard while actively feeding, close inshore or over sand or mudflats in estuaries and creeks. Apart from eels, which are common prey, they take mostly flatfish, flounders and dabs. The popular assumption that they are greedy birds is unfair – they eat a conventional amount, perhaps a sixth of their body weight a day. And although they can look surprisingly clumsy when they're swallowing their catch, they are wonderfully well designed for their job. The tongue has a surface on which rasps point backwards, ensuring a one-way action in which the fish is encouraged towards the throat. The cormorant will arrange the fish so that it slips down head first, shaking it about or even throwing it in the air so that any inconvenient spines

Adult cormorant in winter plumage

will be laid back in repose. The gullet is a flabby tube, capable of great expansion; when the fish is sliding down the bird may look as if it is swallowing a balloon. Yet while the digestive juices are getting to work, and even before the fish gets to the grinding mill of the gizzard, the bird has no difficulty in breathing. Its windpipe is an elastic tube that is stiffened by rings of cartilage, rather like a flexible vacuum-cleaner pipe, and these rings protect the windpipe from pinching or collapsing, so a constant air supply is maintained. The pipe won't kink when the bird's supple neck is twisting and turning, either in feeding or preening.

The catch is brought to the surface to swallow, behaviour which led to domestication of these birds by wily fishermen. Tethered to a bow-perch by lines attached to leather collars round their necks, domesticated birds brought their catch back to their owner because they were unable to swallow them. This method of fishing was perfected by the Chinese, who still demonstrate their skills for tourists, but the practice was even known in Britain, where fishing with trained cormorants was once a regular sport. In the time of James I (1566–1625) there was an official 'Master of the Cormorants' in England. In the mid-19th century, the Rev F O Morris wrote of cormorant-handling in his partwork *British Birds*:

'Young cormorants become perfectly tame, and are readily trained in this country, as well as in China, where, as is well known, the practice is a regular and established one, to catch fish for their owners, the precaution being taken of placing a ring round the neck of the bird, to prevent the prey from being totally swallowed. I was invited once or twice the last few years by my friend Captain Arthur Brooksbank, of Middleton Hall, to go with him and Captain Salvin, to see the tame cormorants of the latter thus fish in the Driffield streams below Wansford in my former parish of Nafferton, and was able on one of the occasions to accept the invitation. A sight well worth seeing it was.'

Cormorants are not beloved of anglers, and are much persecuted wherever fishermen perceive them as overly successful competitors. But in reality their normal catch is non-commercial. Where fish are provided in unnatural superabundance, for instance at fish farms, cormorants inevitably take advantage, but this does not prove that trout and salmon are their everyday fare.

The quantity of nitrogen-rich excrement produced by cormorants can be so impressive that it becomes a commercial proposition to market it as fertiliser in the dessicated form 'guano'. The Cape cormorant of South Africa and the guanay cormorant of Peru both contribute significantly to their nation's economies.

In breeding, cormorants are socially inclined; their colonies, on cliff slopes, ledges or in bushes and trees, may involve dozens of families. They blossom into ornamental plumage at the onset of breeding, with white chins and cheeks and white thigh bars, but without the crest of a shag. Their nests are made of sticks or seaweed cemented with faeces, often decorated with freshly picked flowers or some plastic trifle collected on the beach. They breed in their third or fourth year, laying from two to six eggs which are incubated by the warm-blooded webs on the feet, since they have no brood patch (gannets and shags use the same method).

Cormorant chicks are fed twice daily, when the chick puts its head well inside the parent's throat, inducing it to regurgitate a rich mess of half-digested fish. Apart from fishing sessions, cormorants spend most of their time ashore, carefully choosing undisturbed, slightly elevated positions for the time-consuming business of wing drying, oiling and preening. They are gregarious birds, and not only at the breeding site, choosing to gather together at well-established roost places.

SHAG
Phalacrocorax aristotelis

'Shag' is an Old English word for 'tuft', and the breeding crest of this bird certainly fits the description. This species is superficially similar to the cormorant but smaller and more elegantly slender. In adult plumage it has an oily green sheen (it was known at one time as the 'green cormorant'). The famous crest is erected only for the breeding season. As with both cormorants and gannets, the sexes are alike in terms of plumage.

In habitat and behaviour, shags are more seamanlike than cormorants – they are comfortably at ease in a moderate blow. They are mariners, at home in both inshore waters and offshore, coming ashore mainly for the breeding season to colonise coastal cliffs and islands, with a particular fondness for dark caves and fissures. They rarely show themselves in estuaries and generally only appear inland as a result of foul weather.

As fishermen, shags dive for their catch of wrasse or pollack, or the occasional crustacean, by either leaping in the air to jackknife down or by sliding quietly under

Length
65–80cm

Wingspan
90–105cm

How to
tell cormorants
from shags

Cormorant

Shag

Cormorants are
significantly larger, a
couple of inches taller
and never have a crest.
Shags have a crest in the
courting season, and
their beaks are markedly
slender. Less heavy
around the head, they
also have a shorter, more
snakelike neck. But if
all else fails, count the
number of tail feathers –
cormorants have 14,
shags 12. In family
parties, the juvenile
cormorants can be
distinguished by their
white fronts whereas
in the shags these are
much browner.

the surface if they already have something of a payload in their hold.

Shags are less sociable than cormorants, especially outside the breeding season, but in early spring they will join a loose colony, sometimes close but more often at a distance from their nearest neighbour. They choose less open sites than cormorants, preferring the shade and shelter of overhanging ledges and fissures, especially caves. The nest may even be low down and close to the sea. Both parents collect material such as seaweed and bracken, and line a cup with grasses and decorate it with flowers. The clutch of anything from one to six eggs, but more usually three or four, will be laid as early as the end of February and incubated for a month or so. They are typically aggressive in defence of the nest, with a spectacular yellow gape and dramatic hissing if you approach too close.

Unusually for birds, but as for gannets and cormorants, shags have no bare brood patch with which to warm their eggs, but their circulation system provides a rich supply of blood to their feet. So the shag actually stands on its eggs, covering them with its warm paddles, before settling down to incubate. The young are hatched blind, naked and helpless, remarkably reptilian in aspect, but soon grow a dense black down which sheds as the juvenile plumage appears. A couple of times a day they are fed with a rich and thick soup of well-digested fish which is regurgitated by the parent in response to the purposeful exploration of its gullet by the chick. They become independent at about ten weeks of age, but join with the progeny of other nests in flocks which may involve dozens of birds, often gathering on rocky ledges to socialise. Sometimes the parents may venture to bring up a second brood in the same year.

Once fully fledged, juvenile birds are likely to 'go foreign', adventuring across the Channel or the North Sea to spend their adolescence on the coasts of Brittany or Norway, before returning in due course to their home coast. Grown-up shags are sedentary birds, well distributed around the western coasts of mainland Britain and Ireland, though there are outposts in eastern Scotland and the Farne Islands.

DUCKS

Sea-ducks enjoy feeding in sheltered coastal waters outside of the breeding season. Shy birds, seldom coming ashore, they group together on the water in rafts which may contain hundreds of birds. They are divers, swimming to the sea-bed for molluscs and crustaceans in dives which usually last about half a minute.

EIDER
(Cuddy duck)
Somateria mollissima

A heavily built diving duck, the eider is a handsome, black-and-white bird. In profile both sexes have strikingly wedge-shaped beaks and heads, where the tip of the beak slopes up to the top of the head without a curve. Eiders come from the Arctic, breeding extensively in Iceland and Scandinavia but reaching down to northern Britain and the Low Countries and steadily expanding their range.

Eiders are coastal sea-ducks that breed close to the

*Length
50–71cm*

*Wingspan
80–108cm*

The familiar name 'cuddy duck' comes from the association with St Cuthbert, an early saint who offered the ducks sanctuary on the Farne Islands off the Northumberland coast of England, where he established the first nature reserve in the world. He had a special affection for eiders which thus, in the 7th century, became the first birds in the world to be given formal protection.

water on islands along low-lying rocky coasts, sandy shores, estuaries and sea lochs, and even occasionally by rivers. They arrive at their breeding grounds in early spring. Generally colonial, they make a saucer-shaped nest on the ground, starting with vegetation and lining it generously with down feathers pulled from the female's own breast and flanks. The nest is often in the lee of a feature such as a rock or tideline debris. Usually four to six eggs are laid in early April or May in the south, or even later further north. Eiders often associate their colonies with aggressive species like gulls or terns, to benefit from their protection from predators. But this has not protected them from the depredation of human collectors, who have harvested their eggs in large numbers and semi-domesticated them in order to take the down from the nest lining.

Eider incubation lasts about four weeks, the female doing all the work. The drake leaves her to it when she settles to the eggs, joining a sociable flock with other males for the moult. On hatching, the ducklings are led by the duck to the sea, where they in turn join with others in large nurseries, while the female moults and fattens for the lean days of winter. Highly gregarious birds, they spend much of the winter at sea in flocks which may number in the thousands.

Eiders are coastal diving ducks, diving in shallow waters to a depth of 3m, depending on a supply of littoral crustaceans and molluscs to nourish them. They are especially dependent on a supply of mussels, which they tear from the rocks, though they also take some crustaceans and sea urchins.

EIDER DOWN
Eider down has excellent insulation qualities, allowing eggs to hatch in Arctic conditions. In spite of legal protection elsewhere, farming of down is still pursued in Greenland and Iceland for export to European markets, with an annual take totalling some 250,000 nests. Traditionally the Inuit in Greenland made shirts from the skins of the ducks, needing 15–20 skins to a shirt.

LONG-TAILED DUCK
(Old squaw)
Clangula hyemalis

red-breasted merganser

The appellation '*Clangula*' in the scientific name comes from the latin '*clangor*' for 'noisy', which is certainly true of this duck. At the breeding grounds they indulge in wild aerial displays when the drakes belt out a lusty 'ack-ar-de-lak'. But even in the winter, when we are most likely to see them (*hyemalis* is Latin for 'winter'), and especially on a calm day, you may hear them yodelling, bringing a touch of the Arctic to the south. Long tails are, not surprisingly, the chief characteristic of this sea-duck. Plumage is black, chestnut and white in summer.

Historically, long-tailed ducks are known to have bred in Orkney and Shetland in the early part of the 20th century, but their stronghold is further north. In the breeding season their distribution is circumpolar in the high Arctic, congregating around small tundra

Length 38–41cm (Length including tail 58–60cm!) Wingspan 73–79cm

Old squaws are hunted by shooters on their migrations in Canada and North America. A freshly killed long-tailed duck is said to contain 1mg of vitamin C in every 100mg eaten!

pools, boggy places, and rivers, rarely far from the sea and especially in rocky fjords. Loosely colonial at their breeding sites, they choose a natural depression among vegetation on open ground. Six to nine eggs are laid as soon as the site is ice-free in May/June, and incubation by the female lasts 24–29 days. Ducklings leave the nest soon after hatching, to be taken to a freshwater pond and subsequently to sea. Fledging lasts 35–40 days.

Food is whatever is on offer in the local pool, but on the coast they take molluscs and crustaceans, sea urchins, small fish and some vegetation. They are expert divers, reaching depths of at least 30m, though normal dives are less than 10m and last an average of 30–60 seconds.

After the breeding season long-tails migrate south to become wholly maritime, wintering at sea around the coasts of northwest Europe, mainly in the Baltic but with fair numbers off the east and southeast coasts of Britain, mostly offshore in large rafts. There may be thousands in the Moray Firth and Orkney. At this time these neat little diving ducks exhibit striking plumage. The drake is white with dark brown patches on either side of the neck and an unmistakable grey area around the eye. The female is a duller bird, with mottled, grey-brown upperparts and white underparts, but also with the tell-tale patch around the eye, though rather whiter than in the male.

Male and female greater scaup may be seen among rafts of wintering sea-ducks.

Courting is a winter activity, most of the birds having paired before the northward migration in April. Drakes toss their heads in display, varying the performance with a 'toss and tail-up' when they kick out and lift their after parts right out of the water, their long tails pointing to the sky. There have been sporadic attempts at breeding in Scotland in the past, and it is even possible that they have attempted to nest more recently in the Hebrides.

COMMON SCOTER
(Black scoter)
Melanitta nigra

The common scoter is a compact and glossy black sea-duck. In the drake, even the bill is black, relieved by a yellow patch on the top, which is prominent only at short range. The duck is browner, with a pale patch at the side of the head. Scoters are shy. On the water they have a buoyant posture, but when alarmed they are able to sink down and make themselves inconspicuous. Markedly gregarious on the water, they tend to be in close-packed rafts well offshore. In a raft of common scoters there may be a velvet scoter (the large bird) or, if you are lucky, a surf scoter, with its conspicuous white patches on the beak and above the eye.

*Length
45–54cm*

*Wingspan
79–90cm*

Scoters are shallow-water divers. Their main food catch is marine snails – cockles and mussels – but they will also take crustaceans and some small fish.

This sea-duck may be common by name, but it is decidedly uncommon as a breeding bird in the British

Male and female smew may be seen hugging the sheltered coastlines in winter.

Isles and Ireland. Perhaps some 150 pairs breed in the extreme north of Scotland and around remote lakes in Ireland. The nest is a saucer of grasses lined with down, established within a few metres of freshwater lochs on moorland or tundra. Six to eight eggs are laid in late May or early June. They are incubated by the duck alone, who then sees them through the fledging period of 45–50 days till they go to sea.

It is in winter that the scoter almost deserves the name 'common', for 30,000 or so winter around most of the coasts of Britain and Ireland, being less abundant in the southwest. Augmented by visitors from northern Europe and Iceland, the rafts gather offshore, but not far from the coastline. In flight, common scoters fly low, in long straggling lines.

Common scoters are probably in decline as a breeding species, mainly because of the eutrophication (over-fertilisation) of freshwater lakes and predation by mink.

Length 52–59cm

Wingspan 90–99cm

VELVET SCOTER *Melanitta nigra*
Larger than the common scoter, the velvet scoter has an even more wedge-shaped profile and conspicuous white wing patches. In British waters it appears mainly as a winter visitor. Occasionally it has been suspected of breeding in the far north, but without proof to date. Scan a wintering raft of common scoters and there may be the odd velvet version amongst them, easily noticed because of its larger size.

Length 45–56cm

Wingspan 78–92cm

SURF SCOTER *Melanitta perspicillata*
Surf scoters breed in North America, but they are a more or less regular accidental winter visitor to the British Isles, mostly to Ireland and Scotland. The drake has conspicuous white marks on the bill and above the eyes.

RAPTORS

Raptors – birds of prey – are diurnal carnivores, hunting live prey, though they are not above taking carrion. Typically they have strong feet with which to grab and kill, while powerful hooked bills are used for tearing at prey. The males are usually smaller than the females. They are superb fliers. Eagles are very large; falcons small to medium sized.

WHITE-TAILED EAGLE
(Sea eagle)
Haliaeetus albicilla

Our largest bird of prey, and the only one with an all-white tail in its adult form, the white-tailed eagle is a vulture-like bird with a huge bill and a long neck. It looks massive in flight, with broad, rectangular, deeply fingered wings and a white, wedge-shaped tail. It's fairly widespread along the coasts of the Russian Arctic, Scandinavia (but not Svalbard), Iceland and southwest Greenland (as well as the Middle East and Eurasia). The species was once widespread in Europe, too, but suffered persecution on account of its supposed predation on lambs. In real life it seems likely that, although they occasionally took advantage of a sick or newborn lamb, this has never been a significant activity. Stories of young babies carried off by sea eagles were part of the folklore of remote areas, but there has never been much evidence for this.

As a consequence of persecution, these splendid birds became extinct in the British Isles in the early part of the 20th century. But, buoyed by changes in public attitudes and perceptions, a brave programme of re-introductions was begun when, in 1959, Norwegian eaglets were flown by the RAF to the island of Rum in the Hebrides. Subsequent years brought more young birds, which were released after

Length
70–92cm

Wingspan
200–245cm

'It is impossible to conceal the fact that if the present destruction of eagles continues we shall have to reckon this species among the extinct families of our feathered nobility.'
R Gray, 1871,
London

an acclimatising period in captivity. The first, unsuccessful, attempt at breeding was recorded in 1983, but successful fledging two years later was followed by others. There may be a dozen mature pairs now, with a precarious foothold on several Hebridean islands (though, sadly, not on Rum).

These sea eagles show a preference for small islands in sheltered waters with plenty of fish. Eyries are often on a large tree or a cliff ledge, and although rarely on the ground, they're never very high up either. They have several nests, used in rotation, which are bulky structures built of sticks by both sexes, several feet high, lined with an egg-cup of moss, lichen and other greenery. One to four eggs, although more usually two, are laid in May and incubated by both parents for 34–46 days. Once the eggs are hatched, the male does most of the hunting while the female guards the nest and chicks. Chicks need 800gms of fish daily. Fledging takes 70–75 days.

Sea eagles are opportunist feeders, taking advantage of carrion or following fishing boats for by-catch and offal. But mainly they catch their own fish, hovering or swooping and relying on surprise. Some 90% of their prey is fish-related (for instance dogfish and lumpsuckers); the other 10% consists of birds, birds' eggs and the odd small mammal. Diving ducks such as eiders, and also auks, are harassed by the eagle, which, in forcing them to dive continuously, weakens them till they are easy prey. They also rob the catch of other birds such as gulls, ospreys and peregrines, and may even take fish from an otter.

Sea eagle, from an 8th-century manuscript. Corpus Christi collection, Cambridge.

In medieval times the eagle symbolised the evangelist St John. But subsequently it suffered greatly, persecuted as 'vermin'.

PEREGRINE
Falco peregrinus

Length
39–50cm

Wingspan
95–115cm

A stocky falcon with a short tail and a prominent 'moustache', the peregrine is as powerful as it is compact. In flight its wings are broadly based but sharply tapered towards the tips. The female is significantly larger than the male, or the tiercel.

The peregrine's name means 'wanderer' – apt, as they are widely distributed from the tropics to the Arctic. After the catastrophic declines of the 1950s and 60s, when one of the effects of agricultural pesticides was to cause peregrines to produce eggshells so thin that they broke easily in the nest, they have now recovered spectacularly. The British and Irish population is in the region of 1,500 pairs, which are well established around traditional coasts.

With dashing flight and pointed wings, peregrines are superb in courtship, when the birds indulge in high circling, figures-of-eight, looping the loop, synchronous rolls and talon-grappling – all part of aerobatic pair-bonding. They tend to occupy the same hunting territory every year on return to their breeding grounds, but may well choose a new nest-site, usually in open, treeless country, such as coastal cliffs, crags, quarry walls, ruined towers or an old raven nest. Recently they have taken to even more bizarre sites such as pylons, cooling towers, warehouses and even the windowsills of high-rise flats. They make a mere scrape on a convenient ledge, which may well be decorated with a pile of racing pigeon rings, evidence of their preferred prey. Clutch size is usually three to four. The eggs are incubated for 28–32 days, and the fledging period is 35–42 days. The chicks are heavily dependent on their parents for a couple of months, brooded by the female while the tiercel hunts and provides most of the food. Young birds learn their trade by attacking flying insects before they graduate to sterner prey.

'Man has emerged from the shadows of antiquity with a peregrine on his wrist. Its dispassionate brown eyes, more than those of any other bird, have been witness to the struggle for civilisation, from the squalid tents on the steppes of Asia thousands of years ago, to the marble halls of European kings in the seventeenth century.'
Roger Tory Peterson

The peregrines' coastal eyries are carefully chosen for their strategic overview of the wetland and coastal hunting grounds: traditional sites which may have been occupied at least as far back as the Middle Ages. Their diet consists largely of other birds, usually taken in the climax of a spectacular dive, in which the soaring bird 'stoops' from a great height, almost vertically and at great speed, on to its prey in a partially closed-wing power dive. It may reach a speed of nearly 200km/h, and it actually makes a howling noise as it dives, which must be the last thing a pigeon hears before it is knocked senseless. Choice of prey depends on what's about, and can be anything from a puffin to a goose, but feral pigeons are preferred items. (Racing pigeons frequently retire from the race on crossing the Channel after continental release and on passage to their home lofts in England, taking up residence and breeding on coastal cliffs, where they happily resume the lifestyle of their rock dove ancestors and become a prime target.) The catch is usually taken to an established plucking place. At sea this may well be the crosstrees of a yacht or the truck of a mainmast.

Peregrines continue to suffer greatly from the activities of egg collectors and those who trap live specimens illegally for falconry.

WADERS

The waders (shorebirds) represent a large group of families which mostly congregate on marshes and estuaries. Although some species, like oystercatchers, sandpipers and sanderlings, are seen on sandy beaches, only one can properly be called a sea-going bird – the grey phalarope.

GREY PHALAROPE
(Red phalarope)
Phalaropus fulicarius

*Length
20–22cm

Wingspan
37–40cm*

The illustration shows this bird in its winter plumage, for that is the only way we're likely to see it around the coasts of the British Isles, but its summer condition is so unusual that it is worth knowing something of its breeding behaviour.

Of the three species of phalarope, the grey (known confusingly as the red by some North Americans, presumably because they are more familiar with the bird in its red-breasted breeding plumage) is a true mariner and the only wader which commonly swims. Its dense plumage and a layer of down that traps air next to the skin enable it to float like a cork on the surface of the sea. It is superbly adapted to the aquatic life, with lobed webs on the toes, as in the unrelated grebes. It is a fearless bird, with a surprising indifference to human approach. Yet another surprise is that in the breeding season the female is larger and much more colourful than the male. In breeding plumage the female has a white face with a dark crown and yellow beak, its upperparts are boldly patterned and its underparts a striking, dark chestnut. The male is dowdy by comparison, an indication of the untypical breeding strategy of this species, where traditional roles are reversed and the female is the dominant partner in courtship and copulation.

Grey phalaropes sometimes congregate to take advantage of the oily secretions of a whale's breath (or that of a common porpoise, as here), or take parasites from its back. In the past, flocks of phalaropes led whalers to their prey.

Grey phalaropes are circumpolar in their summer distribution, common along the high and low Arctic coast. On arrival in May or early June they wait at the edge of the sea-ice for a thaw to reveal the ground on the nesting areas. At this time they have empty stomachs after the long haul of migration and are quick to take advantage of the burgeoning insect larvae and small invertebrate organisms of pools, shallow inshore waters and the tideline.

They are loosely colonial and non-territorial at the breeding grounds, the season starting in early June in Iceland and Svalbard, and later in Arctic Russia. The chosen sites are on marshy tundra or small islands in areas having plenty of freshwater ponds with abundant vegetation. Both sexes make several nests that are always close to water, forming neat cups with available materials. The female makes the final choice of nest. Courtship is initiated by the female and the pair bond lasts just long enough for her to provide her mate with a clutch of three or four eggs, which it then becomes his job to incubate. The female promptly abandons him to join a club of other females and non-breeders of both sexes off the coast (although often enough she will take the opportunity of mating with another male and providing him with a clutch to incubate).

Incubation, for 18–20 days, is entirely the responsibility of the male, who, in order to be inconspicuous at the nest, has suitably dowdy plumage. He starts incubation when the last egg has been laid by the female, so the chicks are born more-or-less simultaneously. Vulnerable to predation at the nest, they leave as soon as they have hatched out, in the care of the male. The female plays no part in their upbringing.

Grey phalaropes feed on insect larvae and other small aquatic organisms, wading along the edges of pools or swimming in tight circles like a spinning top, to encourage food items to the surface, where they are picked off daintily with their thin, pointed bill. As soon as the young can fly, the family party goes to sea.

Females migrate south in mid-July, and the males with their brood follow later. The most oceanic of the phalaropes, they move far south from the polar breeding grounds to winter at sea on the plankton-rich waters off West Africa. But as passage birds they may be seen in British waters, normally well offshore, from late September to November. Less commonly, they appear, sometimes even in large numbers, on shallow fresh waters. In a storm they may even appear inland. They are markedly tame. Insubstantial birds they may seem, but in fact they happily endure most rough seas, riding high in the water.

SKUAS

The name 'skua' comes from the Icelandic *'skufr'* and is presumed to be a rendering of their chase-calls in flight. Long and dark, skuas look superficially like immature gulls, but they are heavier, more robust and menacing in mien, as befits a bird of prey. Theirs is a piratical nature and they have hawk-like beaks to serve it.

Their bills are stout, hooked and plated, with a soft fleshy section at the base of the upper mandible. They have long wings, with conspicuous white patches at the base of their primaries, stout legs and webbed feet. The larger species, the great skuas or bonxies, have longish square tails. The rest, smaller and known as jaegers (from the German, 'hunters'), have wedge-shaped tails with two extra-long central feathers. Their flight is gull-like, but faster and with more powerful drive, and a curiously stiff, gliding effect on the wing-beats.

Skuas range the open oceans but are birds of moderate to high latitudes at breeding time. True seabirds, they come ashore only to breed. They nest on the ground on tundra or islands at the extremes of latitude in both hemispheres, sometimes far from the sea. They are monogamous, pairing for life. The nest-site is often chosen to be conveniently near the food supply provided by a ternery or gullery. It is not an elaborate affair, just a hollow lined with a bit of greenery. They return to the same nest every year, and maintain a touching relationship with the nearby larder – one pair of skuas to one hundred pairs of gulls, for instance – an arrangement which tends to long-term stability for all the members of the club. Skuas are not sociable in the usual seabird manner, though there may be a fair number breeding in the same area. There are usually two eggs, the chicks being highly dependent until they are fledged; the parents are very aggressive in defence of the nest and young and will unhesitatingly attack any unwelcome visitors, including humans.

As birds of prey, in the breeding season skuas feed on small mammals, large insects, eggs and chicks of other birds. They are kleptoparasites – carnivorous buccaneers – at sea, forcing terns, shearwaters, gulls, phalaropes and even gannets to disgorge their catch, often grabbing it before it reaches the water. They will settle on the surface for carrion and will follow trawlers or whalers for offal and other ships for galley waste. Great skuas sometimes even roost on board a vessel.

All skuas are long-distance travellers, wintering in the opposite hemisphere from that in which they nested. They may also range far over the polar ice.

POMARINE SKUA

Stercorarius pomarinus

Length 46–51cm, including tail streamers

Wingspan 113–125cm

'Pomarine' is the shortened form of 'pomatorhine' – or 'lid-nosed' – as this bird has its nostrils partly covered by a scale. In fact that is a description that applies equally to all the skuas and distinguishes them from the gulls, but time has given the corrupted form of the name only to this particular species.

The pomarine skua is smaller than the great skua but larger than the other long-tailed skuas, and is decorated with strikingly long, blunt and spoon-shaped twisted tail feathers. Both sexes look alike, with a dark crown and golden yellow sides to the head. It is polymorphic, in two colour phases; either all-brown or brown with white underparts. The lighter phase outnumbers the dark by 20 to one. A thickset and powerful bird, its flight is slow and purposeful, with steady wing-beats. It is often seen following ships, especially trawlers.

Pomarine skua tail

The pomarine skua is circumpolar on the Arctic coast, preferring low-lying tundra with freshwater pools. It is not common in Greenland or Svalbard. It rarely, if ever, breeds in the British Isles.

Both sexes choose their nest-site and make an insubstantial ground nest – a shallow scrape, if anything, with possibly a few scraps of moss or

vegetation. Two eggs are laid and incubated by both parents for 23–28 days. Chicks usually leave the nest after a few days but stay in the area. They are fed by regurgitation. They fledge in about five weeks but are dependent on their parents for a couple of weeks more before they are able to fly independently.

At nesting time the abundance of lemming prey is a prime factor in breeding success. In a poor lemming year skuas may choose not to attempt breeding. But they will also take the eggs and young of other birds.

Outside the breeding season they are ocean wanderers, truly pelagic species perfectly able to cope with foul conditions and specialising in areas of strong upwellings with their abundant surface life. They fish by dipping to grab from the surface.

ARCTIC SKUA
(Parasitic skua, Richardson's skua)
Stercorarius parasiticus

Arctic skuas chasing
a young kittiwake

*Length
41–46cm
including
tail streamers*

*Wingspan
97–115cm*

As with the pomarine, the Arctic skua is polymorphic with two colour phases, light and dark, the lighter form having a dark breast band and becoming commoner further north. Its main distinguishing feature is the central tail streamer, which is shorter than that of the long-tailed skua. Arctic skuas have been seen only a few miles short of the North Pole, and are known to call at remote camps on the Greenland ice-cap to beg for scraps. Smaller than the great skua and the pomarine, they are the commonest skuas of the west Palaearctic and are circumpolar in distribution, from well above 80° down to 57° north. The dark form, more or less uniform brown, is the most typical of the British Isles, where it is at the southern limit of its range.

Arctic skuas breed on hilly moorland and wetland in Shetland and Orkney, and less commonly in the Hebrides and the far north of mainland Scotland. They are usually found in single pairs but sometimes in loose colonies, in close association with auk or kittiwake or tern colonies, since these provide abundant food in the form of half-fledged chicks at a convenient time in the nesting cycle. They prefer a dry nest-site amid swampy ground. The pair bond is strong, and is probably for life. They usually breed for the first time in their fourth year. Commonly two eggs are laid in June, incubated by both sexes for 24–28 days. The young leave the nest soon after hatching and are fed by both parents. They defend their nest territory vigorously, intruders being dealt with by a graded sequence of reactions which depend on the perceived danger. They perform a distraction display which feigns injury – one wing drooping pathetically as they 'struggle' to lure the intruder, perhaps a man or a fox, away from the nest or chicks. The bird stumbles along the ground, squealing and holding out a 'broken' wing, only to take off and fly boldly away once the intruder is at a safe distance. If the interloper goes closer to the nest or chicks the intensity of the display is doubled, and as a last resort the other parent will stoop from the air in a powerful attack, to the extent of tearing a man's scalp. Always do what the 'injured' bird asks – that is, walk towards it and therefore away from the chicks it is protecting.

Arctic skua tail

Both parents care for the young until well after fledging. The young birds start to fly in about four to five weeks, fed on a diet of half-fledged auks, terns and kittiwakes whose colonies are nearby and provide easy pickings.

Outside the breeding season, Arctic skuas are fast, piratical predators, forcing gulls and terns to throw up their fish catch. They winter at sea off the coast of West Africa.

LONG-TAILED SKUA

Stercorarius longicaudus

Length
48–53cm,
including tail
streamers

Wingspan
105–117cm

A small, lightly built version of the pale morph of the Arctic skua, the long-tailed skua, perhaps not surprisingly, has strikingly long and slender middle tail feathers which may seem as long as the rest of the body. The crown is a more clear-cut black than that of the Arctic skua, and the breeding adult lacks the breastband. Flight is more graceful and buoyant than in the Arctic skua. There is a dark morph, but it is rare. Distribution of the long-tailed skua is circumpolar in the Arctic tundra, from northern Canada by way of Greenland, Iceland, Svalbard and the coast of Siberia. They are scarce passage-migrants in Shetland and the Hebrides, with a few appearing on both the east coast of England and the west coast of Ireland.

In loosely knit colonies on high tundra and scree, pairs form soon after arrival at the breeding grounds in May. The territory contains a lookout point located on a hummock or similar high point. The nest is in a shallow depression on the ground, perhaps on a raised peat mound or amongst stony scree. Long-tailed skuas are less enthusiastic for small islands and skerries, and often nest well inland. The nest is usually unlined.

Two eggs are laid in June or early July. Both parents incubate, but the male does most of the hunting, bringing prey to the nest, where he skins and tears it apart and shares the food. The incubation period is 23–25 days. Breeding success is dependent on a healthy population of lemmings and other small mammals, though long-tails have been known to take advantage of fish refuse and offal at a human camp. The female does most of the brooding and feeding of the chicks, while the male hunts and defends the territory. Two days after hatching the chicks leave the nest to hide in vegetation, running to the parents when they fly in with food. After a week or two they begin to tear their own morsels. Fledging takes 24–26 days. Their main prey is lemmings and other small mammals, comprising 90% of their diet, which is topped up with birds, fish, insects and even berries.

Long-tailed skua tail

Both adults tend the chicks for about three weeks after fledging, when they all leave the breeding grounds. The chicks will not return till they breed in their third summer.

Like the Arctic skua, these birds are pelagic outside the breeding season, feeding on marine fish, and wintering far out to sea as far south as 50° north in the Atlantic.

GREAT SKUA
(Bonxie)
Catharacta skua

Great skuas chasing a young gannet

Length
53–64cm

Wingspan
125–140cm

'Bonxie' comes from the Norse *'bunksie'* – meaning 'dumpy body'. The great skua is indeed like a big stocky herring gull, but dark brown all over, with conspicuous tell-tale white flashes on the wings and a short tail. Its flight is heavy and rather laboured, except when it is engaged in piracy, when it chases fish-loaded birds with relentless purpose, agility and speed, forcing them to disgorge or drop their catch.

The most widely distributed of the skuas (a very close relative breeds in the Antarctic) the great skua has been established for a long time in Iceland and northern Britain. It extended its range both north and south in the 20th century.

As summer visitors, something like 8,000 pairs of great skuas breed in Shetland, Fair Isle and Orkney, with smaller numbers on St Kilda and the outer

Hebrides and the mainland Scottish coast, sometimes as a lone pair and sometimes in a small colony. There may be many non-breeders in the vicinity. They defend their territory with vigour. Their chosen site is mostly on small islands or upland tundra close to rocky coast. There is always a convenient lookout which serves as a loafing or roosting site. The nest is made in heather or rough pasture – a meagre scrape with scant lining. Both sexes, but mostly the female, incubate the two eggs, laid in late May/early June, for 28–30 days. Fledging lasts 42–49 days. The parents are aggressive in defence of nest and chicks, dive-bombing and physically attacking an intruder, whether fox or man, giving a glancing blow with the feet which are lowered at the last moment as the bird attacks from behind. They often draw blood from a scalp wound.

Great skua tail

In the breeding season piracy is less evident, with other birds and eggs becoming important items of prey, gathered from a hunting territory which is distinct from that for breeding. The chicks leave the nest two or three days after hatching, to hide in nearby vegetation and wait for feeding visits by the parents, when they run out to beg vociferously. The young are assiduously cared for by both parents, fledge in six to seven weeks, soon become independent and leave the breeding area to go to the sea. It is here that they learn the trade of a pirate, harrying terns and gulls to relieve them of their catch. Great skuas will also take advantage of carrion and they commonly follow ships, especially if they are fishing. They are fond of communal bathing in fresh water.

They are pelagic in winter, from the Bay of Biscay and south to the waters off West Africa and east as far as the Sargasso Sea.

GULLS

Gulls are opportunist feeders, having a go at anything, and they are the common companions of any coastal sailing expedition. In summer there may be terns fishing the surface waters, too. Common and Arctic terns, with their swallow tails, or sandwich terns, with their heavier bodies and yellow-tipped bills, all patrol the inshore waters, ready to pounce on surface titbits.

Gulls are sturdy and sociable birds with powerful bills, webbed feet, long and pointed bow-shaped wings and fairly short, square tails. The sexes are similar in plumage, immatures tending to a mottled grey-brown, adults becoming more white, grey and black after several years. They nest noisily and colonially, sometimes in large numbers, often in close proximity to a convenient food source. They are moderate to large in size, varying in length from about 30cm to 75cm. They offer a serious challenge in field identification in that they are comparatively uniform in coloration and carriage yet present a seemingly infinite range of subtle variations in plumage. To make matters worse, they may hybridise or wear the white coat of an albino. They are supremely adapted to breeding requirements, nesting anywhere from the Arctic pack-ice to exposed cliffs or seaside rooftops. Opportunist feeders, they are scavengers by trade, enjoying anything from seashore invertebrates to the eggs and chicks of other birds, including those of their own species. Ship's garbage, rubbish dumps, sewer outfalls and lunchtime crusts in the city park are all grist to their mill. Sociable in feeding and at the nest colony, they will even nest happily in company with other species such as terns or auks. Often barely tolerated by some people, they have a high resistance to persecution, although in some species there is evidence of a decline in numbers.

BLACK-HEADED GULL
Larus ridibundus

Mediterranean gull

Black-headed gulls are smaller and more slender than kittiwakes (see page 89), easily recognised in breeding plumage by the chocolate brown balaclava mask and the broad white margin at the forward edge of their narrow, black-tipped wings. They have red legs and bills. In flight, they are graceful and tern-like. More gregarious and somewhat tamer than other gulls, they breed from the Russian steppes and sub-Arctic islands all the way down the coast of northwest Europe and the Iberian peninsula to the Mediterranean. Always within 20 miles or so of the coast, they are associated with the edge of shallow water – fresh, brackish or salt.

Colonies are established all round the coast of Britain and Ireland, though most strongly in the north

Length
34–37cm

Wingspan
100–110cm

Juvenile black-heads noisily beg for food from the parent birds, as illustrated.

and west and not at all in the southwest peninsula of England. On the whole they breed in relatively few places, but in large colonies. The concentrations tend to be low down at ground level or at bush height, very often miles inland around lakes and freshwater lochs, but many are on coastal sand dunes, saltings or low-lying islands.

The nest is a rather perfunctory affair, a shallow scrape lined with available vegetation, sufficient to provide a saucer for the eggs, though it will be built up to a substantial mound in wet conditions. Two to six eggs are possible, but three or four is normal, laid from mid-April. Incubation is shared by both parents for 22–24 days, and on hatching they both feed the chicks, which soon become infected by the general air of excitement and wander about from tussock to tussock. There is an element of danger in this activity, for black-heads are quick to take any opportunity, including a neighbour's fat chick. The young will fly at five or six weeks.

Nineteenth-century egging took a great toll of their numbers. Artificial islands were created to encourage them to nest in places protected from predators and convenient for harvesting. Black-headed gulls are normally single-brooded, but they were susceptible to farming. When the first clutch was taken, it was promptly replaced by the birds. The second clutch, which provided slightly smaller eggs, was also taken, with the birds then allowed to raise a third. Eggs are still collected for food, but nowadays predation by foxes, hedgehogs and mink is probably a more serious threat. Reduced human persecution has released the species to flourish in a marked expansion of numbers throughout the 20th century.

The black-headed gulls' diet consists mostly of animal material, though they will take some vegetation. Feeding inland, they take earthworms and insects and they will harass other birds like lapwings to steal titbits from them. They are especially adept at 'puddling' on flooded grassfields to encourage earthworms to the surface. They commonly hawk for flying insects such as ants or butterflies, continuing well into dusk to chase moths, but on the coast they

Head comparison of black-headed gull in summer (above) and winter plumage

Little gulls. These delightful small birds are often found along the British coastline during the spring and autumn migration.

will go fishing and take crustaceans, molluscs and holidaymakers' sandwiches.

They are resident throughout the year and are mainly sedentary, but after the breeding season, from mid-August, many of them gather on tidal waters along the coast, with a preference for sand or mud (though it has to be said that the easiest place to see them in winter is around parks and lakes in cities like London). Adventurous young birds may reach the Atlantic coast of France and the Iberian peninsula from September. At the same time there is an influx to the UK from the Baltic and Benelux countries. In early spring, passage birds work their way up the east coast to Scotland, the Faeroes and Iceland.

DERIVATION OF 'GULL'

In Latin the ejaculation '*vae*' represented 'woe'! In Old Norse '*vaela*' was 'to wail'. A Welsh version was '*gwelan*'. From this the French took '*goéland*', the Cornish '*gullan*' and the English reduced the word to gull.

HERRING GULL
Larus argentatus

Length
55–74cm

Wingspan
130–158cm

The best-known, commonest and most widespread of British and Irish gulls, the herring gull is the standard 'seagull'.

A large, sturdy and heavily built bird, it is largely white, but the mantle and most of the wings are a pale blue-grey, the dark end of the wing tipped with white spots, known to birders as 'mirrors'. The powerful, hooked yellow bill has a striking vermilion spot on the lower mandible. Pale eyes add to its fierce expression. It has pink legs. The well-known laughing cry is one of the best-known bird calls, a boon to radio dramas needing to indicate a seashore location. Herring gulls are well established around our coastline, though less firmly in the southeast and east. They enjoy strong and buoyant flight, whether soaring or in active flapping.

Their habitat is rocky coasts, estuaries and inshore waters. They venture offshore in company with fishing vessels or in the hope of handouts, but are happiest in sight of land. They are gregarious birds, whether at breeding places, when they are feeding or at roost. They have a habit of perching in the comparative safety of unattended yachts or small boats, leaving unwelcome evidence of their occupation.

Herring gulls are colonial at their breeding station, though single or several pairs are not infrequent. On the whole they prefer grassy cliff slopes, ledges, islands and sand dunes. Over the last half dozen decades they have taken to the artificial version of cliff tops, nesting on rooftops between chimney pots, a choice which has served them well, increasing their numbers in a measure of safety. Aggressive in defence of their territory, they attack people, dogs and cats, disputing ownership of anyone's property – behaviour which brings them into some disrepute. The nest is a substantial mound of grasses and seaweeds, collected by both of the pair and lined with a neat saucer designed to hold two or three eggs, sometimes more. Incubation is by both parents for 28–30 days. The young are well developed when they hatch and leave the nest when a day or two old to skulk close by, fed by both parents. They fly just before they are six weeks old, but continue to beg food successfully long after they have left the nest area. Juveniles are dusky brown, becoming paler in their first summer, much closer to adult plumage in the second summer, and as adult but with a few brown flecks in their third year. Maturity comes in three to five years.

As opportunists, their diet is omnivorous. They will eat anything from fish (with chips), crabs, molluscs, carrion and food waste. They scour grassfields and wet sand, 'puddling' to encourage worms to the surface. They will hawk for flying ants or other insects, and may thieve a cockle or a mussel from the beak of an oystercatcher but then have difficulty in prising the valves apart to get at the juicy muscle inside. Their best party trick is to carry their prize up to a concrete promenade or road, dropping shells from a height to crack them open and get at the contents.

Herring gulls flourished through most of the 20th century as a consequence of protection and a more sympathetic public attitude, and most especially because of the abundance of food provided by fishing activities and rubbish tips. But, more recently, they have been in decline for reasons that are not entirely clear.

They are a somewhat sedentary species, plentiful in winter all round the coast. In winter plumage their heads and the backs of their necks are streaked brown; they have a penchant for seaside towns and fishing ports, where they can rely on handouts from people. At this time there will be a considerable influx of birds from Scandinavia and the near continent. There may also be autumn arrivals along the south coast from the Iberian peninsula of the yellow-legged gull, *L. cachinnans*, a bird regarded until recently as a race of the herring gull.

Common gulls are smaller than herring gulls, and have yellow bills and legs. They breed in Scotland and Ireland and are only relatively common in the south in winter.

LESSER BLACK-BACKED GULL
Larus fuscus

A rather slimmer and less thuggish bird than the closely related herring gull, the lesser black-backed gull has a striking red eye-ring and a slate-grey (not black!) mantle. Both its bill and its legs are yellow, at least in summer. In flight it is skilled and graceful.

As a summer migrant it arrives at the breeding grounds in April, a couple of weeks later than the herring gulls with which it is often closely associated. But the colonies are established on sand dunes or on

Length
52–64cm

Wingspan
128–148cm

the relatively flat ground behind sea cliffs, often amongst heather, bracken or bluebells, rather than on cliff slopes and ledges. Some are inland, patronising boggy moorland. Increasingly they are taking to rooftops of buildings. They are abundant around most of the coast, except in East Anglia and the southeast. The nest is similar to that of the herring gull, being a fairly substantial pile of grasses and seaweeds, but it is placed amongst dense vegetation, never on a cliff ledge. It is beautifully lined with finer grasses, mosses and lichens. The usual clutch is three eggs, incubated by both sexes. On hatching, the chick leaves the dangerously open platform of the nest within a day or so, to crouch in the safety of cover. Fledging takes 30–40 days, and most of the caring is done by the female.

Lesser black-backs are opportunistic feeders, just like herring gulls. At sea, they plunge-dive on fish shoals, often in large flocks. They will also work over a beach or rough grassland for invertebrates, and they show ever more interest in rubbish dumps, taking advantage of the wasteful habits of man. They often roost on reservoirs.

Nowadays, many winter around Britain and Ireland, but the traditional wintering grounds are in northwest Africa.

Much persecuted in the 19th century, their populations increased greatly under protection and as a result of the decline of traditional game-keeping. Their numbers were so healthy in the middle part of the 20th century that conservationists culled them in the interests of other species, such as shearwaters. But over the last few decades they have gone into serious decline. In Orkney and Shetland this is probably due to the increase of the predatory bonxies, but the reasons elsewhere are not so clear. Since Britain and Ireland hold 40% of the European population, there is some cause for concern.

GREAT BLACK-BACKED GULL
Larus marinus

Great black-backed gull chasing a puffin

A very large and intimidating gull, the great black-backed gull has a black back and a big head housing a strongly hooked and massive bill. The flesh-coloured legs are shorter than those of the lesser black-back. Flight is ponderous, with slow wing-beats. The white 'mirrors' at the end of the black wings are more conspicuous than on the lesser black-back. Somewhat arrogant birds to our eyes, they have a deep voice, barking a repeated 'ak-ak-ak', amongst other calls, in proclaiming ownership and dominance of their chosen breeding territory, on the top of sea cliffs and rocky islands. They are found all around our coasts except for those of eastern and southeast England.

Length
64–78cm

Wingspan
150–170cm

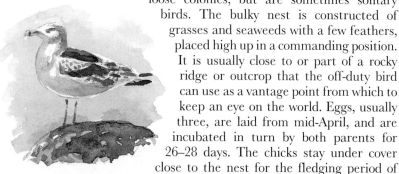

Young great black-backed gull

In the breeding season they tend to occur in loose colonies, but are sometimes solitary birds. The bulky nest is constructed of grasses and seaweeds with a few feathers, placed high up in a commanding position. It is usually close to or part of a rocky ridge or outcrop that the off-duty bird can use as a vantage point from which to keep an eye on the world. Eggs, usually three, are laid from mid-April, and are incubated in turn by both parents for 26–28 days. The chicks stay under cover close to the nest for the fledging period of seven or eight weeks, unless they are disturbed. But long after they have flown, the chicks continue to beg for food.

Great black-backed gulls are omnivorous, but their speciality is in the taking of eggs and other birds. They will lie in wait for puffins and shearwaters returning to their nest burrows at dusk or leaving at dawn, killing the prey by stabbing and shaking. Thus torn apart, often all that is left of the unfortunate prey is an inside-out skin. Puffins are even taken in flight, caught by the neck and carried to the shore to be eviscerated. Great black-backs also catch mice, voles and young rabbits. Carrion includes dead lambs and grey seal pups. The nest area will be littered with pellets revealing the nature of their catch.

In winter the gulls are widely dispersed, though they are mainly resident. Their numbers are increased by incoming winter visitors from Norway. At this time they are as likely to be seen on muddy coasts and estuaries as on inshore waters. Once much persecuted as a predator but also for glass-case trophies, they have benefited from legal protection since the end of the 19th century, and are doing well except in those places where they face competition from the even more successful bonxies.

KITTIWAKE
Rissa tridactyla

The only ocean-going gull, the kittiwake has a slender lemon-yellow bill, short black legs and a demure black eye, which gives this delicate bird a less loutish appearance than most gulls. There are no white tips to the wings, whose ends appear to have been 'dipped in ink'. Graceful in flight, the kittiwake bounds along with a fast and buoyant action. Its call is pleasantly onomatopoeiac – 'kitty-way-ake'. Juvenile birds have a strikingly attractive plumage in which the wings display an 'M' mark. This was their undoing back in the 19th century when their wings were sent to London for the fashion trade at a time when it was the done thing to wear part of a dead bird in your hat.

Kittiwakes enjoy a strong pair bond and are colonial nesters, from a couple of dozen pairs to a seabird city of thousands. They frequent rocky coasts with precipitous cliffs wherever there is suitable habitat

Length
38–40cm

Wingspan
95–110cm

round the coasts of the British Isles. In the breeding season home is a sea cliff or cave, sometimes on impossibly precipitous faces. Where there are settlements, they may nest on buildings, piers or warehouse window ledges (the industrial equivalent of a cliff face). In fishing-boat harbours they will nest on the tractor tyres used as fenders on the docksides. The nest is a carefully constructed and compacted mass of mud, seaweed and assorted vegetation, with a neatly excavated cup to hold the eggs. On the narrowest ledges they will cantilever it out to create more space, when it then overhangs a sheer drop. The advantage of these seemingly perverse locations is that they offer protection from marauding foxes.

Kittiwakes, unlike other gulls, enjoy bathing in fresh water, indulging in communal flights to a pond or lochan or temporarily flooded grass fields.

Usually two eggs are laid in late May or June, and incubation is performed by both parents for 26–28 days. The newly hatched chicks are programmed to sit very still, for if they were to walk about they would be in danger of falling from a great height to a certain death. (Most chicks leave their ground nests – which are dangerous because they attract predators – a couple of days after hatching, to lie camouflaged in the greenery while their parents forage for food.) The chicks are fed by both parents. Feeding is by regurgitation at the nest, an adaptation to the confined space which requires the chicks to sit tight. The birds defaecate carefully over the edge of the nest, with the result that there are conspicuous patches of white below, leading to a healthy growth of scurvy-grass.

Kittiwakes take a variety of food, from fish (by way of shrimps) to marine snails, terrestrial invertebrates, plants, grasses and seeds. They pick food from the surface or plunge for it in tern fashion, sometimes immersing themselves completely. They are confirmed ship-followers, hoping for galley waste and enjoying the plankton thrown up by the ship's screws. As scavengers they will follow a trawler in the hope of offal and will congregate around whale blows to enjoy

Young Sabine's gull. Storm-driven migrants may appear off the southwest coast in late summer/early winter. An elegant small bird, it has a conspicuous wing pattern that is somewhat similar to that of a juvenile kittiwake.

breathy globules of grease. They forage far out at sea, sometimes in very large flocks.

The chicks are guarded continuously till they are three or four weeks old. They fly at about six weeks. After their first flight, they may return to the nest for a few days for last feeds from their parents. At the end of the breeding season, the entire population often takes off for a mass silent flight as dawn breaks and the light improves. Very soon the nest ledges are deserted.

They winter far out at sea. Birds resident on the British coastline will be joined at that time by immigrants escaping the rigours of an Arctic winter. In spring and autumn large numbers of 'foreign' kittiwakes will visit British waters on passage to the breeding grounds in Iceland and other points further north.

There has been a marked increase in kittiwake population in the last hundred years, a consequence of legal protection and a more sympathetic public attitude to birds in general. This is especially true of the southeast of England, where new colonies have been established. On the other hand, the northern population in Shetland has suffered over the last couple of decades, partly because of problems with the availablity of sand eels, but also on account of predation by the increasing numbers of bonxies, or great skuas.

SALTY PROBLEMS

Divers, gulls and seabirds in general have a particular problem when it comes to dealing with the quantity of salt which they inevitably ingest in both drinking and fishing. They absorb far more than is healthy for them and more than their renal system can deal with. The surplus salt is conveyed by a network of blood vessels into fine tubes connected with the nasal glands. This concentrated sodium chloride is in solution and drips constantly from the end of the beak.

TERNS

There are over 40 species of tern inhabiting the seven seas. Most are birds of the coast, though some are oceanic and some are inhabitants of freshwater marshes. They are smaller, more graceful and more streamlined than the gulls which they superficially resemble, and they have narrower, more pointed wings and slender, pointed bills. Many have deeply forked tails, earning them the sailor's name of 'sea swallow'. They are short in the legs with small webbed feet, and are buoyant on the sea, yet rarely in it, for they swim poorly. They may enjoy a rest on a piece of driftwood or raft of seaweed.

Terns tend to have white bodies with grey backs and wings, and very often have a black cap, and sometimes a jaunty crest. Their bills and feet range in colour from black to blood-red or yellow. Exceptionally aerial, they roost at night but are in the air for most of the day outside of the breeding season. They can live for long periods on the wing (tropical sooty terns fly continuously except at their breeding time). They fly with steady, purposeful wing-

Sandwich tern

beats, never soaring and tending to look down, their beaks pointing to the water. In searching for fish they may hover, then plunge head first for small fish at the surface – splash, snatch and up again.

Typically, terns nest in close-packed colonies, some of them very populous indeed. The stimulus and noise of company leads them to synchronise their egg-laying, with resulting advantages in terms of safety – the safety of numbers which confuses predators. Even so, there is high mortality, which accounts for the average clutch of three or four eggs in many species, compared to the single egg of, say, the sooty tern of tropical waters which only rarely appears around the British Isles and suffers less from predation.

COMMON TERN
Sterna hirundo

Common terns are summer visitors to most of our coast, but not to south Wales or the southwest of England, and are much less common in the far north. The distinction between this species and the Arctic tern is not easy, leading to the birder's fudge of identifying 'comic' terns. But if you're close enough to get a look at the black tip of the coral-red bill, you know you have a common tern. Also, if you're looking

Length 31–35cm, including tail streamers

Wingspan 82–95cm

up at the bird from underneath as it flies by, the outer primaries of the common tern are relatively dark whereas all the primaries of the Arctic tern are uniformly pale, almost translucent. The legs of the common tern are significantly longer than those of the Arctic. Both have the deeply forked tails which give sailors the right to call them 'sea swallows', but these are somewhat longer in the case of the Arctic tern.

This is the commonest tern around the southern half of Britain and if the current decline of the Arctic population in Scotland continues it will soon be the most common in both Britain and Ireland. Like other seabirds, terns benefited greatly from the protection begun in 1869 when the Sea Birds Protection Bill outlawed egg-collecting and shooting for sport, but they have lead a chequered existence since then and their populations are anything but stable.

The 'kee-rah' or 'seeee-gull' alarm call of the common tern greets any intruder to the colony, but they have various ways of saying 'kik-kik-kik', both at the colony and at sea. They are wildly aggressive in defence of their breeding territory, attacking intruders by dive-bombing and, in the case of an unprotected head, tearing at the scalp and screaming in anger; walk into a tern colony at your peril! Pugnacious birds, they will fight amongst themselves for the choicest nest-sites.

Common terns are gregarious birds, both on fishing excursions and at their breeding place. Their colonies are generally established on the low-lying coasts of rocky islands, sand dunes, shingle spits and gravel pits (and on gravel banks in Scotland). Early in the season, they indulge in a curious behaviour known as the 'dread', when for

Black terns may be seen as passage birds on migration.

no apparent reason the entire congregation takes off and flies noiselessly out to sea, only to return again soon after. The provision of man-made nest-sites on lagoons and freshwater ponds in the form of 'scrapes' and artificial islands has been a great success in giving them some protection against predators. They will normally have paired before they reach the nesting grounds but courting continues with highly ritualised displays first in flight and then on the ground. The prospective pair engages in a charming courtship display: the male dances up to his fancy, who begs for the fish he presents. He gives it to her, she takes it and then he begs for its return. They tend to come back to the same site every year, which is usually little more than a shallow depression, a mere scrape, often without any lining, or perhaps with a few items of vegetation or tideline detritus. Three eggs are usually laid in mid-May, although two or four are also common. Both birds take it in turns to incubate for 21 to 23 days. The newly hatched chicks stay in the nest for three or four days, then leave to skulk nearby, staying still to rely on their camouflage in case of disturbance. The chicks are fed on whole small fish, such as sand eels, which may be longer than the chick itself, so that while the head end is being digested the tail hangs out for all to see. They fly at about a month old, and are sexually mature in their third or fourth year.

Their diet is mainly of marine fish, taken close along the edge of the shore. Typically they prey on small fish, principally sand eels, but also crustaceans, insects and assorted invertebrates. They hover before plunge-diving, bringing the catch to the surface to swallow it on the spot, unless it is destined for the chick back at the nest, when a single fish is carried. Breeding success is heavily dependent on the supply of suitable fish. Predators like rats, mink, skuas, gulls, crows and even owls take a heavy toll. Sometimes a particularly high tide will create havoc. The chicks are dependent on their parents until long after they have fledged, but if they are lucky they may live to the ripe old age of 30.

At the end of the breeding season, even as early as July, but mostly in August/October, the families leave to work their way around the Iberian peninsula to the wintering coasts of West and South Africa.

ARCTIC TERN

Sterna paradisaea

*Length
32–39cm
including
tail streamers*

*Wingspan
80–95cm*

As summer visitors, Arctic terns breed on the Farne Islands off Northumberland and in Anglesey, but are found mostly in the west and north of Scotland and western Ireland. The high Arctic is the usual breeding stronghold of this bird, but its breeding range reaches south just as far as the British Isles. In the recent past, this was the commonest tern in Ireland and Scotland.

During breeding it has a dark crown, while the rest of the plumage is a light grey, with longer tail streamers than the common tern. The short legs, feet and bill are a dashing scarlet. It hovers to plunge-dive for small fish, like sand eels, in deeper water and further offshore than the common tern. (In the Arctic it will hover and pick insects off the tundra exactly as it hovers and snatches small fish from the sea.)

Birds arrive at the breeding area in May, choosing the same sort of habitat as the common tern, though with less emphasis on inland locations. They are even more aggressive in defence of the nest than the common terns. If you are foolish or cruel enough to walk into an Arctic ternery, prepare to be attacked mercilessly. They will not hesitate to mount a spirited offensive, diving fearlessly and screaming as they come close, drawing blood from an unprotected scalp. The prudent tern-watcher, even if he stands at a reasonable distance, should carry a lofted stick, held high, for the tern will always attack the highest point of an intruder. Generally speaking, it's best to leave them in peace after admiring their mastery of aerobatics from a distance.

Roseate tern

Arctic tern populations have endured something of a roller-coaster existence, with drastic changes in fortune from year to year. Recently they have been suffering even more than usual, with massive failures in breeding in places like Shetland, possibly as a result of fluctuations in the sand eel population. At the moment their long-term prospects do not look good here, at the very southern end of their range.

Little tern

Towards the end of August they leave on their amazing migration, a long-haul flight across the whole of the Atlantic to the other side of the planet, where they winter in the Southern Ocean and amongst the pack-ice in Antarctica's Weddell Sea. This is believed to be the greatest migratory movement of any bird – they enjoy a life of perpetual summer.

Arctic tern

AUKS

Guillemot

Razorbill

Puffin

Auks are found almost entirely in the colder waters of the northern hemisphere (they are replaced in the southern hemisphere by penguins and diving petrels, to which they are not related). They originate from and are most numerous in the North Pacific but are well represented in the North Atlantic and the Arctic Ocean.

Medium-sized birds, they are mostly dark above and white below. The sexes are similar, to our eyes at least. They have dense waterproof plumage, often with brightly coloured bills and face parts, and with plumed ornaments about their heads. Their heads are large; their bills long and slender to short and blunt. Their legs are placed well aft on a chunky body, with a short tail. They are divers and swimmers, using their short, paddle-like wings to whirr in the air. It's something of a compromise, as they don't fly as well as gulls or dive as well as penguins. Their flight is direct and somewhat desperate, but fast and furious. On the whole they prefer to move about by swimming, and by 'flying' underwater, in hot pursuit of small fish and plankton.

Auks swim with great skill. It is not easy to catch fish underwater, but they are well adapted. Their plumage is compressed and their bones are more solid then in terrestrial birds, so that they are not carrying excess air down with them. Their ribcage is strong to withstand the increased pressure. In diving, they hyperventilate, then breathe out as they jackknife. While breathing is suspended, the heart beats more slowly, so reducing energy requirement.

The larger auks (alcids), like the puffins, feed on fish; small ones, like the auklets, on plankton. As true seagoing birds, they come ashore only to breed. At their breeding places they congregate in noisy clusters, standing upright in penguin fashion, a stance which we find endearing. Some breed sociably, in huge colonies of many thousands, some in scattered groups, and some alone. They nest in a variety of situations: high up on mountainous scree slopes inland; on precipitous sea cliffs or grassy cliff-top slopes in burrows; or in tree holes or on tree branches. Some even patronise artificial nestboxes. Most make no formal nest but drop their egg or eggs on the bare rock or on to the soil.

Auks winter at sea in small or large flocks, normally not too far from the coast. At this time those with bill sheaths lose them through moulting. At sea they float high like gulls, but are more squat in shape. It has to be said that they are not easy to spot at sea, though they are among the commonest birds in the northern hemisphere. There are literally millions of pairs of puffins and guillemots and other auks. But there are also elements of decline as a result of several factors, which include oil and chemical pollution, disturbance, and the increase in fishing activities by their primary competitor, man, which affects the abundance of prey species as well as trapping large numbers of birds in fishing nets.

BILL ADAPTATIONS

The auks show a wide range of bill adaptations unusual in a single family. This is carried to the extreme in the puffin, with its highly decorative coloured bill, which is cone-shaped in profile and flattened vertically; during underwater pursuit it is able to catch and hold between ten and 30 small fish in one load for its chick. The roof of the mouth and the tongue are grooved with small projections (called retroverted papillae) pointing inwards, which assist retention of the fish caught during the underwater chase.

GUILLEMOT
Uria aalge

*Length
38–45cm*

*Wingspan
64–73cm*

Over a million guillemots inhabit the British coast, and 150,000 around Ireland; they are the most numerous of our auks. Of the two races, the Scottish is significantly darker than the more chocolate-brown-coloured southern bird. The bill is slender and pointed, gannet-like for grasping a single fish longer than its bill. 'Bridled' individuals have a white, orbital eye-ring with a white line extending back. They are rare in the south, perhaps occurring as 1% of the population, but further north the percentage gradually increases to maybe 25% in Shetland.

Adults remain close to the coast all year, but may visit the breeding cliffs from December, though they come ashore towards the end of March in the south, and later in the north.

Why 'guillemot'?
The derivation of the name guillemot is controversial. It comes from the French, without much doubt, and is said to be a pet form of the Christian name Guillaume, or William. Early English names for the common guillemot were Willock, Willick or Willy. But another possibility is that it comes from 'goéland' ('wailing' in German) with the addition of 'moette'. Moette is from the old German, found today as möwe, or gull. 'Mew' is of course an old English word for gull. Guillemot may therefore be translated as 'wailing gull'.

Guillemots find their food in dives which may last over a minute and reach down as deep as 60m. They will normally swallow their catch before surfacing, unless they are taking it back to their chick. Sometimes a group of birds will join together in a line to circle and herd a shoal before picking off the fish at the edge.

Guillemots breed on ledges on vertical or near-vertical cliffs on the rocky coasts of offshore islands and stacks. Colonies may consist of more than a hundred thousand pairs, densely packed in a 'seabird city'. Guarding the smallest breeding territory of any bird, they stand close together, often literally shoulder to shoulder with their neighbour, on noisy and crowded open ledges. On stacks, they will crowd together on the flat top in such numbers that there is a virtual carpet of birds.

Courtship is a very public affair; when one pair starts, everyone joins in. The result is that all members of the colony tend to lay their eggs at the same time, so the birds act almost with a single purpose, sticking close together in order to fight off predators and to benefit from group strength. They make no attempt at building a nest; the single, pear-

shaped egg is laid on bare rock, and held between the feet of the incubating parents, who share responsibility. Incubation takes 28–36 days, and the newly hatched chick is fed by both parents, with single fish carried back to the ledge head-first in the bill, pointing forward. The chicks huddle together on their precarious ledge, never walking more than a few token inches. A general raucous growling is characteristic of a guillemot colony, interspersed with the wistful and plaintive calls of the chicks.

At nearly three weeks of age, on a calm evening towards dusk, the chick takes the plunge and flutters down at an angle to belly-flop into the all-embracing sea, closely followed by its father. They swim out to sea as the chick learns its trade as a diver. (The few birds left behind are likely to be snatched up by the constantly watchful gulls, ravens and jackdaws.) In high summer it is a common sight to see a proud parent with its somewhat smaller chick in tow. Able to fly at about two months, it is attended by the male for another month. When they part, the young chick, like

Of guillemot ledges: '…although every place affording a foothold is crowded to excess, the utmost order and decorum everywhere prevail; each seems desirous of assisting and accommodating the other.'
T R Jones, 'Cassell's Book of Birds', 1867

The American version 'murre' for the common and Brünnich's guillemots derives from its original usage in southwest England for the razorbill, Alca torda, a species also known in Wales as 'morr'. This name, which is clearly onomatopoeic, was first recorded in Devon and Cornwall by Ray in 1662.

Aran islanders of the west coast of Ireland ate guillemots on a Friday and in Lent, claiming that as they never flew over land and ate fish they could be regarded as fish.

many an adolescent, will explore something of the world. The female will stay around the nest-ledge for a further few weeks, but by mid-August the seabird city will be deserted.

In winter guillemots become much whiter round the chin, cheeks and throat. They tend to remain at sea around the British Isles, though the juveniles may venture as far as continental coasts from Norway to Portugal.

Guillemots suffered much in the past from large-scale domestic egg-collecting and from 'sport' shooting, which devastated the east coast colonies, particularly at the turn of the 19th and 20th centuries. They tend to make their dispersal movements in winter by swimming rather than flying, so are particularly vulnerable to oil pollution. Oil is less of a threat today, but birds are still caught and drowned in fishing nets. Although there are fewer colonies nowadays, their population is increasing.

GUILLEMOT EGGS

Guillemot eggs are pear-shaped, or pyriform. This is assumed to be an adaptation which makes them less likely to fall over the edge. In a somewhat explosive experiment carried out in 1948, a Russian scientist called Uspensky fired a series of shots deliberately to disturb a breeding colony of Brünnich's guillemots. Early in the season, this resulted in a cascade of eggs falling from the ledges. But later in the season, though the birds took fright and flew off the ledges, 'not a single egg tumbled off the ledge'. Freshly laid eggs, Uspensky concluded, roll off the ledge. But as they are incubated and the embryo develops, the air space expands at the larger end, thus shifting the centre of gravity to the pointed end, causing the egg to spin rather than fall when disturbed. So the egg is most likely to come to grief at the early stage of incubation, in which event the female simply replaces it.

RAZORBILL
Alca torda

Razorbills may be confused with the similarly sized guillemot, but they are slimmer and have a deeper, laterally compressed bill which is crossed by a vertical white band – strikingly reminiscent of an old-style barber's razor. They all have black upperparts and relatively large heads. The British population is nearing 150,000, and the Irish 35,000, the sum of which is probably 20% of the world population. They are well distributed around the coasts of Britain and Ireland except for the coast south from Yorkshire and clockwise as far as Hampshire.

Length 37–39cm

Wingspan 63–68cm

These are birds of inshore waters, first collecting near the colony from January, enjoying communal courting displays at sea before coming ashore in late March or in April. Once ashore, their courtship becomes more personal, involving bill-touching, neck-nibbling and a performance in which they rustle their wings and rattle their bills as castanets, growling and grunting in accompaniment.

The loosely organised colonies are found on steep sea cliffs and boulder-and scree-strewn slopes, and are sometimes close to guillemot colonies, although razorbills prefer less open sites. Often they choose protection from skuas and gulls in the shape of a roof over their heads, in a cavity, under a boulder or in scree.

Their breeding behaviour is similar to that of the guillemot, but they have different nest preferences. Whereas the guillemots nest shoulder-to-shoulder on exposed ledges, razorbills are more inclined to hide themselves under boulders, or to half-hide in crevices and corners. They may go for holes in scree-slopes or group themselves amongst boulders. Nonetheless, if the country suits them, they may be present in fair numbers. Like that of the guillemot, the nest consists more of a site than a construction, but there may be a few token pieces of vegetation, or a couple of stones alongside the egg. Being less densely populated on the ground, razorbills suffer more than guillemots from the attentions of gulls, but seem able to fend off jackdaws. Both parents incubate a single egg for 32–39 days, and, as with the guillemot, the chick leaves the nest soon after its second week, to follow its male parent to sea.

Food is mainly in the form of small fish such as sand eels, but crustaceans, molluscs and marine worms are also eaten. The razorbill's wedge-shaped beak grasps and holds several small fish at the same time. Fish are caught by surface-diving, often after the bird has dipped its head underwater to scan for prey. Unlike the guillemot which catches fish one by one, razorbills may grab several, carrying them back to the waiting chick across the bill instead of along it. In Norway it is said that they underfly puffins and snatch the sand eels from their beaks, while off the Pembrokeshire coast they even chase puffins underwater.

The winter movements are as for the guillemot, though young birds may venture further south, often as far as the Mediterranean, northwest Africa and the Azores. Some French birds may visit our coastal waters in winter. Razorbills suffered from egg-collecting in earlier decades, but they are now probably on the increase.

GREAT AUK
(Garefowl)
Pinguinus impennis

Woodcut by Thomas Bewick, from his 'History of British Birds', Longman, 1847

The great auk is – sadly – extinct, serving today as a cautionary tale. It was a giant razorbill, the largest of the auk family, once well established and breeding on both sides of the North Atlantic and around western and northern coasts of the British Isles. Channel Island middens were found to contain great auk bones carbon-dated to 20,000 years ago. They existed in the Mediterranean till at least the Bronze Age. They probably bred in gregarious communities, almost shoulder-to-shoulder like guillemots, on rocky islands.

Like the penguins of the southern hemisphere, to which they were not related, great auks travelled the evolutionary route to flightlessness. As superb divers, they found fish prey without difficulty. Their wings were reduced to paddles because they had no need to fly. However, flightlessness became their undoing: explorers and fishermen found them a convenient source of food, since they were so easy to catch.

Height
75cm

Wingspan
50cm approx
(wing 16cm)

'God made the innocence of so poor a creature to become such an admirable instrument for the sustenation of man.'
Richard Whitbourne, 1622

105

'PENGUINS' OF THE NORTH

The original English/Welsh name for the great auk was 'penguin':

> 'Madock ap Owen Gwyneth [a 12th-century Prince of Wales] gave to certain islands, beasts and foules, sundry Welsh names, as the Island of Pengwin . . . there is likewise a foule in the said countreys called by the same name at this day.'
>
> R Hakluyt, *Voyages*, 1589

In Willughby's Ornithology', published in 1687, the extinct bird we now know as the great auk was captioned 'penguin'. The assumption is that the word variously formed as penguin, pingouin, pingüim, comes from the Latin 'pinguis', meaning 'fat'.

Later it became known as 'garefowl', which comes from the Norse *'geirfugl'* – a name given by the Vikings when they first encountered it in Scotland in the 8th century. Possibly it was something of a joke, a perverse reference to that superb flyer the gyrfalcon. The pioneer Basque whalers called the great auk *'grand pingouin'*, easily corrupted to penguin. There are also several Penguin Islands off Newfoundland, so-called because they were once great auk strongholds.

It is a reasonable assumption that the southern hemisphere penguins got their name by way of the earliest Portuguese seamen when they discovered the jackass penguins of South Africa and explored southern South America to find the Magellanic penguins. They transferred their auk version *'pingüim'* (the name of the only flightless bird they knew) to this newly discovered family of flightless birds with an upright posture. Elizabethan explorers like Drake and Hawkins brought their version, 'penguin', by the same route. The northern hemisphere auk family, however, whose members seem today to be on the evolutionary road to flightlessness, is not related to the penguin family. The similarity between them is a classic example of convergent evolution, in which animals which have the same mode of life tend to look like each other even though they are not related.

> 'Its wings are very small, and seem to be altogether unfit for flight.'

Although once abundant, they were over-exploited for their meat, eggs and feathers, and for bait. Large, tasty and present in good numbers on easily accessible islands, they were taken in ever-increasing quantities by local fishermen and longshoremen, then by European sealers and fishermen who travelled to the Newfoundland cod-banks from the 16th century. It is said that British and French fishermen herded them on to their boats for slaughter. They were probably already in decline by 1700, by which time they were confined to a handful of colonies in northern Canada.

As they became uneconomical from the fisherman's point of view they became more valuable as glass-case specimens for the casual collector and as museum specimens. Ironically the great auk's very rarity caused it to be hunted with ever greater zeal for 'academic' collections. The market value increased and the remaining breeding sites in Iceland were systematically raided in the 1730s and 40s. On Funk Island, Newfoundland, the last individual was collected in about 1800; the last Irish bird from Great Saltee off Waterford in 1834; and the last survivor on St Kilda from Stac an Armin in 1843. The last of all was taken from Eldey Island, off the south coast of Iceland, in 1844, to join the dodo as little more than a pathetic memory.

Museum specimens can be seen in the University Zoological Museum in Cambridge, in the Zoological Museum in Oslo and in various other places, but many are taxidermists 'mockups'.

'Their food was fish and crabs. They made no nest, but laid their single egg upon the bare rock. Nobody knows what their exact breeding season was, though they were found with eggs in June and young in July; nobody knows how long they incubated their single egg, or how long the young stayed on the breeding rock before it swam away. The Garefowl ... laid its egg on low rocky islands and skerries, on to which it could struggle and waddle at any state of the tide. All its known breeding places were lonely and remote; they were all in the...colder waters of the North Atlantic, though not, as is popularly supposed, in the Arctic.'

James Fisher

BLACK GUILLEMOT
(Tystie)
Cepphus grylle

Length
30–32cm

Wingspan
52–58cm

Smaller and plumper than the common guillemot, this bird is uniformly black, but with its conspicuous white wing-patches and vivid red legs it is unmistakable. In the British Isles it is at the southern end of its breeding range. It is circumpolar in distribution, breeding in Arctic Canada (where it is known as the sea pigeon from its habit of laying two eggs), Greenland, Iceland, Jan Mayen, Bear Island, Svalbard and points east to Siberia. Residential and sedentary by disposition, its stronghold is in the north and west of Scotland, most especially in Orkney and Shetland, but there is also a respectable population in the Isle of Man as well as a few in north Wales and an increasing number around Ireland.

Black guillemots arrive at their breeding grounds to nest in May/June, favouring rocky coasts, small islands, sheltered sea lochs and bays. Less gregarious than other auks, they may be in a loose colony of a few birds or a few dozen. Easy-going in their choice of nest-sites, they lay their eggs directly on to a shallow depression in a hole or crevice in scree, or under stone slabs, boulders or driftwood behind the beach. They will patronise a man-made site, a hole 'improved' in a harbour wall or pier, or the space under a conveniently placed fish box. They may even explore sand martin excavations. Unusually for an auk, they lay two eggs. Both sexes alternate shifts in incubating the two eggs for more than three weeks, then care for the chicks which sit tight in the hole till they fledge in another five weeks. They are independent soon after.

Black guillemots are shallow-water fishermen. Less sociable than other auks, they often hunt alone, but may join with others to form line-abreast on the water to herd fish. Strings of black guillemots are not uncommon, sometimes in impressively straight lines. They are strong swimmers, with a preference for shallow water, diving in the top ten metres to search the bottom for fish like butterfish, blennies and lumpsuckers, but also crustaceans and molluscs. On average they will be on the surface for 15 seconds before diving for as long as a minute, during which time they may have travelled as far as 75m; they may dive as deep as 50m. Taking fish back to the chicks, they carry them whole in their bills.

In winter, they lose the white wing-patches and become much less conspicuous, though the red legs remain. Sedentary by nature, they do not travel far, staying close to the colony throughout the year, though birds from the more rugged and stormy areas like Fair Isle tend to gather in more sheltered inshore waters.

Winter plumage

LITTLE AUK
(Dovekie)
Alle alle

Length
17--19cm

Wingspan
40--48cm

About the size of a plump starling and even smaller than a puffin, the little auk has a tiny bill and a bull-like head on a compact body with short tail and wings, appearing almost frog-like. While it normally winters in the far north, close to the pack-ice, many come south and winter off the North Sea and northern Atlantic coasts of Britain and Ireland. It is the most abundant of auks, but the stronghold of its breeding range is above the Arctic Circle. In Greenland there are well over a million breeding pairs and in Svalbard well over ten million. With a probable world population of 30 million, it is in competition with Wilson's storm-petrel for being the world's most numerous seabird.

Little auks breed in the high Arctic. They are extremely gregarious, gathering in great rafts of many thousands inshore, taking off for mass aerobatics, almost darkening the sky, before coming ashore to their nests.

Colonies are established near to areas of high plankton production, not far from the edge of the summer pack-ice and always in places where there is open water, at least when the young are due to hatch. Large colonies are established, usually on an open sea-face, either on frost-shattered scree slopes or in fissured cliffs, from sea level up to a few hundred metres. They prefer a gentle slope, offering easy take-off from their vantage points in rocks above their nest holes. There is a great deal of chatter and gossip at breeding time, when off-duty birds spend a lot of time resting and preening on these vantage points. Disturbed by an intruder or a passing piratical gull, they erupt as a dense flock in a 'dread', sweeping over the hillsides with a curious laughing cry in a manoeuvre which presumably serves to confuse the predator. The resulting showers of droppings fertilise a luxurious growth of lichens and mosses. The area below a little auk colony is always marked by lush plant life: a Svalbard colony of 70,000 pairs is calculated to benefit the land beneath it with 60 tonnes of faeces per square kilometre during the breeding season. Mosses, lichens, scurvy grass and chickweed grow in abundance, in turn attracting herbivorous birds like ptarmigan. Early Dutch whalers collected the scurvy grass and ate the leaves, raw or boiled.

The insubstantial nest of small stones with a bit of lichen or grass is well hidden in a crevice or under a boulder. A single egg is laid in late June or July and incubation is by both sexes for something over 24 days, when the chick is close-brooded for a few days before being fed by both parents. The breeding season is timed to coincide with the seasonal peak of plankton and small fish. Little auks specialise in taking copepods, amphipods and other small items from the plentiful zooplankton of midsummer. The total harvest for a typical colony of 100,000 breeding pairs may amount to over 70 tonnes. Mostly the birds fish within a couple of kilometres of the colony, but may be as much as 100km out to sea. They fish at night, when prey migrates to the surface, and carry it back to their chicks in a throat pouch.

Little auks take copepods when they come to the surface at night, stowing large numbers in their throat pouch, in order to carry them back, hamster-style, to the waiting chick.

On emerging from the safe nest, fledging after about a month, many of the young are taken by glaucous gulls or foxes. Parents and surviving young leave together for the sea where the adults endure a flightless period while they moult.

In autumn the Svalbard population of little auks moves south to the Norwegian Sea or across to southwest Greenland. Some of these birds penetrate as far as the British Isles, which represents the southern end of their wintering range, though individuals may reach the coast of Iberia. Normally they remain well out at sea, unless foul weather deprives them of the chance of feeding and they drift or are blown downwind, ever hungrier, on to a lee shore. In severe weather fair numbers are recorded off Shetland. Apart from those in Orkney and Shetland, most coastal sightings are recorded between October and February on the east coast, and also around the sheltered waters of west Scotland, while the odd individual may turn up almost anywhere. Most amazing of all is when stormy weather causes a major 'wreck' of little auks. Driven ashore, sometimes in huge numbers, settlements and cities far from the sea become invaded by the bizarre sight of these tiny birds stumbling along the streets, dazed by the lights.

In winter, when they are most likely to be seen in British and Irish waters (see illustration page 110), the sides of the neck and throat are white, but the stout little bill is unchanged, whereas the young puffin with which it might be confused has a longer bill. Young guillemots and razorbills are much bigger.

FOOD FOR THE INUIT

The Inuit of northwest Greenland are highly dependent on little auks for food in summer, when their coast is ice-free and they are unable to hunt for seals and whales. The birds are captured in flight by sweeping a 'flegg-net' attached to the end of a long pole. They are eaten raw or boiled; in the case of baked birds, they are eaten whole. It is also said that they can be enjoyed after they have spent a couple of months fermenting in a blubbery sealskin sack. The Inuit also wove shirts from the skins, in the days before cotton underwear arrived on the scene in the 20th century.

PUFFIN
(Sea parrot, sea clown)
Fratercula arctica

Puffins have a stout body, a parrot bill (in summer) and dapper plumage set on top of orange webbed feet. They are everyone's favourite, yet most people never see one in the wild and when they do they are surprised by its diminutive size. Unmistakable at close range, the puffin is not so easy to identify in poor light and at a distance, when it is easily mistaken for one of the other auks. This species is confined to the North Atlantic (other puffins are found in the North Pacific); its world stronghold is Iceland. They are established on the Lofoten and Faeroe Islands but are most easily seen on the seabird islands of northern Britain: the British and Irish population is not far short of a million birds. Very few are found in the southwest of England,

*Length
26–29cm*

*Wingspan
47–63cm*

PUFFLING?

'Puffling' was originally the name given to the cured carcass of the fat Manx shearwater fledgling, which was taken in large numbers for market. From medieval times until the end of the 18th century it was an esteemed delicacy in Britain. The young shearwater was corpulent or puffed up, hence the name 'puffling'. It is not so clear how the word came to be applied to the sea parrot, as our *Fratercula arctica* ('little brother of the Arctic') was known till well into the 19th century. Maybe it found its way back from the English markets to the Celtic seabird islands of Wales to be confused with the sea parrot which, like the shearwater, also nested in burrows. The scientific name of the shearwater is still *Puffinus*, just to add to the confusion!

fair numbers are found off Wales and southern Ireland, while many more can be seen in the Hebrides and in Shetland. On the eastern side of Britain they are well established on the Isle of May, and there are colonies on the Northumberland Farnes and at Flamborough Head in Yorkshire.

Puffins are true seabirds, coming ashore only to breed in early April, choosing the grassy slopes on the top of remote islands. Gregarious birds, they nest in sociable colonies. During the day there is not much activity in the area, but towards evening the puffins muster in large rafts close inshore, taking off to perform spectacular flights round and round the bay before plummeting in to land near the nesting area. The circling is an anti-predator stratagem, confusing the great skuas and great black-backed gulls which attack them in flight. The male puffins are the first to make a cautious landing on the breeding slopes, the horny sheaths on their bills at their most parrot-like and colourful. Prominent grooves in the orangey-red parts of the bill betray their age: they have two when they are sexually mature (sometime between two and four years old); any more than two indicates that they are more than five years old. Breeding first at the age of about four years, they must find a nest-site and court a desirable female. The heaviest and most experienced puffins bag the best sites, underground in burrows either of their own making or in holes which rabbits or shearwaters have conveniently prepared.

The puffinry is set amid huge cushions of thrift and luxuriant growths of red campion which flourishes on

'The puffyn hatcheth in holes in the cliffe, whose young ones are thence ferreted out, being exceeding fat, kept salted, and reputed for fish as coming nearest thereto in their taste.'
Richard Carew,
Survey of Cornwall,
1602

the nutrient-rich bird dung flung liberally about by socialising puffins. However, on some well-manured and trampled patches the ground may be so rich in phosphates and nitrogen that no plants can survive. The most desirable burrows are on the steepest slopes, the advantage being that the emerging bird can become airborne with minimum effort.

Puffins import some grass and feathers to furnish their underground burrows. A single white egg is incubated for 36–45 days, the parents working in shifts. The newly hatched chick is brooded by one parent for a few days but both must soon go fishing, for the chick has a good appetite. The chick is fed on a diet of small fish of sand-eel size. The adults are surface-water divers, swimming underwater down to about 15m. Picking off its first sand eel from the shoal, it grips the head firmly between the back of its tongue and the serrations on the bottom of the upper mandible. Subsequent fish are grabbed from left and right and packed from the back, as the tongue progressively bends up and grips head after head, until the beak has a full load of something like 20 (though there is a record of 61) caught in a vice grip. Then it's back to the cliff-top slope, a row of little tails drooping from either side, at random, from the beak. They pose and enjoy the evening air a while before disappearing below ground. The chick stays in its safe underground retreat, totally dependent on the parents which feed it maybe ten times in a day until it is larger than they are, for a variable fledging period of somewhere between 34 and 60 days. Towards the end of that period it is abandoned, to fast for some days before emerging at night to find its own way, fluttering and stumbling, to sea, when hunger forces the issue.

The rich colouring and the horny or fleshy appendages of the adult puffin's bill and face are functional only in courtship display. The decorative basal sheath of the bill, the fleshy mouth rosette, and horny eye-patches are shed after the breeding season.

In winter puffins are comparatively drab in appearance and have a much more conventional shape, discarding the 'clown' image. They winter far out at sea, and may live for 20 years.

Puffins have long been regarded as choice items for the galley and the kitchen. In Iceland, to this day, there is an annual catch of the best part of 200,000. Nowadays it is mainly the full-grown, newly aerial birds which are taken in August by the skilful deployment of long-handled 'flegg-nets'. They are eaten boiled, stuffed, roasted, dried, smoked or salted. 'The Puffin we compare, which coming to the dish, Nice palates hardly judge, if it be flesh or fish.'
Michael Drayton, 'Polyolbion', 1613

FERAL PIGEON
(Street pigeon, homing pigeon)
Columba livia

Length
31–35cm

Wingspan
63–70cm

Sailing, cruising or ferrying in the English Channel in summer, there is always a strong chance of an uninvited but usually welcome guest. Racing pigeons are transported to the Continental coast and released in large numbers to find their own way back to their home lofts in England. Superbly adapted and fed for fitness, they have no problem in finding their way back to the eggs on their nest in double-quick time. Their 'owners' hope for glory when their bird is first back home. But quite often the racers decide that they've had enough sport and they go wild, returning to the coastal cliffs from which, in ancestral terms, they originally came.

Feral pigeons have a fascinating history. They are derived from the purely wild rock doves, which now survive only as a remnant population on the remotest and wildest parts of Scotland and Ireland. But hundreds of years ago they were common coastal birds. Their story is intimately bound up with that of the history of agriculture. Preserving enough food to get through the winter was much more of a problem years ago than it is now. Few farmers could store enough hay to maintain more than a breeding nucleus of cattle, sheep and pigs, and refrigeration was the prerogative of the very few who could afford an ice house. For most people, salted meat was the rule and fresh meat the rare exception. Rock doves – cave nesters – which could almost have been designed for domestication, provided the answer, for some at least. Placid, and with undemanding breeding requirements, their strong suit was a facility to produce fat young squabs at all seasons of the year, by rearing them on pigeon 'milk' (a cheesy curd regurgitated from the crop lining) for the first days of their life before they were able to digest vegetable materials. So it was possible to find fresh meat from a rock dove's nest right through the dark days of winter, a time when no other bird was able to breed. It was very soon realised that, by providing extra ledges, more nests (and thus more squabs) could be encouraged. But coastal caves are often inconveniently difficult of access; before long it was also realised that it would save a lot of trouble if the birds were encouraged to breed in artificial caves inland, in order to spread the delights of pigeon pie to those whose residences were far from the roar of the sea. Thus, dovecotes became established, and highly successful they were in providing the only fresh winter meat until 18th-century man discovered the potential of root crops, which cracked the problem of keeping domestic-fed animals throughout the year.

Today those old pigeon houses stand idle, but the descendants of their occupants are still going strong, as street pigeons and as homers, or racing pigeons. Not infrequently racing pigeons drop out of a cross-Channel race and retire to live on the coast. The result is that, though pure rock doves may be confined to the far north and west, these mongrel pigeons whose

Temporary pigeon guests should be allowed to find their own berth and offered water and some small crumbs of cheese. With luck they will stay a short while and continue their journey, leaving only a reminder of their visit to be wiped away. If you need to release them, try to do it at the coast. If you want to report the visit, tell the Royal Pigeon Racing Association, The Reddings, Cheltenham, GL51 6RN, but they will need to know the ring number.

'Thou dove that art in the clefts of the Rock, in the secret places of the Stairs.' Song of Solomon, 2–14

remote ancestors lived all around the rocky coasts of Britain now carry on the tradition.

Feral pigeons are common all round our coastline, living as their ancestors did, breeding in caves and foraging for seeds on the clifftops. Many of them sport the two black wing-bars and blue-grey plumage of the truly wild birds, but feral pigeons come in every colour, from black to white by way of blues, greys, reds and browns. Although the first generation of cliff colonists may wear a racing ring, their progeny do not, and the cliffs and bays echo to the whirr and clap of the wings of flocks of pigeons that are as wild as anyone might reasonably wish. And although pigeons are famous for their homing ability over great distances, these birds are comfortably sedentary. The peregrines which suffered so badly from agricultural pesticides have taken full advantage of this ready availability of prey. Peregrine nest places are often home to a pile of pigeon rings. Peregrines themselves, of course, have long suffered from the attention of falconers, with the young 'eyasses' taken from the eyrie and trained to hunt. Today, respectable falconers work only with birds which have been bred in captivity.

NOT ONLY PIGEONS AS PASSENGERS...

In high summer there will be large numbers of birds on passage to their winter quarters further south. At this time it is possible for almost anything from a swallow to an osprey to cadge a rest while they are crossing the sea. There may even be butterflies. Painted lady butterflies may arrive to decorate a ship or yacht in their hundreds, resting on their pre-breeding migration across the sea from Spain and France. If they seem to need help you may offer them sugar-water in this classic recipe: half a teaspoon of honey and half a teaspoon of castor sugar to a breakfast cup of water. This may seem a weak mixture but although the insects will eagerly attack a stronger solution it will upset their digestion and shorten their life. Put some of the mix in a saucer and create a cotton-wool island. Introduce a butterfly to the island and it will unroll its tongue and suck up the moisture. If it is really exhausted it may be necessary to use a pin or needle to uncoil the tongue, gently drawing it out and touching it to the damp cotton wool.

SEALS

There are three families in the Pinnipedia (finny-feet). First is the Otariidae, which includes fur seals and sea lions, and second is the Odobenidae, represented by the walrus. None of these occur round the waters of the British Isles, except as very occasional vagrants.

The third major family grouping is of the Phocidae, the 'true' seals which have no protruding external ear, cannot run or raise themselves on fore flippers, cannot swivel their hind flippers and must clumsily haul themselves on land in caterpillar fashion. These are well-represented in our waters by the Atlantic grey and the common, or harbour, seal.

With torpedo-shaped bodies, cushioned and insulated with a thick coat of blubber and dense pelage, seals are superbly designed for fast underwater travel. Their nostrils are closed and sealed by muscular contraction as they enter the water. They exhale before diving to reduce the amount of air in their lungs, and derive the necessary oxygen from their well-supplied blood systems. Their heart-rate reduces and slows, as does their metabolism. Seals are in their element as divers, able to work hard and remain underwater for long periods. They are perfectly able to chase and capture fish in murky conditions; they use a form of echo location similar to that of bats. On surfacing it is several minutes before their heart-rate returns to its surface rhythm.

They are sociable animals, gathering close together in large numbers, sometimes several hundred at a time, in assemblies before and after the breeding season. Away from the breeding beaches, you are likely to see a seal either basking on a comfortable waterside rock, or surfacing between bouts of fishing. If you are lucky, you will see one treading water while it deals with a freshly caught fish, holding it with forepaws while tearing the flesh with its powerful teeth.

Seals must come ashore to breed, but are comfortably able to pup on sandbanks, beaches, caves and even well inland on low-lying islands in the north. Males and gravid females gather annually at their breeding place, to copulate soon after the pups are born. Implantation is delayed for three months so that although the gestation period is nine months the annual cycle is maintained.

Killer whales are their natural enemies, but they have suffered greatly from the depredations of human sealers and from competition with fishermen. Seals have been much persecuted by fishermen who resent their habit of sampling fish in nets, especially as they sometimes damage the nets, but there is little evidence that seals damage fish populations as a whole.

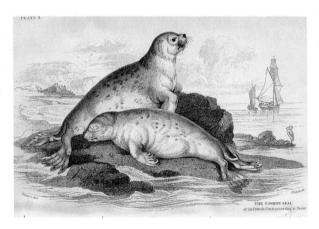

Common seal. Engraving by James Stewart from Sir William Jardine 'The Naturalist's Library', 1839

PLATE 3

THE COMMON SEAL
of the French Coast according to Cuvier

SEAL WORDS

Bull seals collect a **harem** of cows. Newborn seals are **pups** which may join a **pod** of their peers. In due course they become **yearlings**. Immature males are **bachelors**.

In numbers, seals are a **herd**, but at the breeding beaches they become a **rookery**.

COMMON SEAL
(Harbour seal, sand seal, spotted seal, selkie)
Phoca vitulina

Common seals, while overlapping in distribution with the grey in Scotland, tend to go for tidal sandbanks, sheltered lochs and ledges on the eastern side of the country. One of their strongholds is the East Anglian Wash. In muddy and sandy places, their body colour is an effective camouflage while they are in the water, but their porpoising shapes and inquisitive stares usually give them away. They have a short muzzle, appearing puppy-like by comparison with grey seals. Hauled out on remote sandbanks, they give birth to their pups in late May and June. On shore they move in caterpillar fashion, at a disadvantage as they are unable to move fast, but they are never far from the sea, where they are totally at home: fast, and superbly adapted, powered by their hind flippers. Even the newborn pups will swim, close to their mother,

Length
bull 150–185cm
cow 140–175cm

Weight
bull 55–105kg
cow 45–87kg

within a few hours of birth, when the incoming tide covers the sandbank where they were born. Well able to recognise its own mother by both smell and voice, the pup may even climb on her back for a lift. At two or three days old they are perfectly capable of diving to sweep the bottom for whelks, staying down for a couple of minutes. At ten days old they may stay down for the best part of ten minutes.

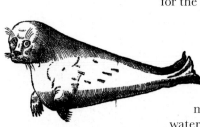

Common seals are expert divers, with powerful hind flippers to propel them deep underwater in search of cockles, whelks and flounders. They have good vision, but an acute sense of smell and hearing is more important to them in the murky waters of the British Isles. In fact they are perfectly able to catch fish in total darkness. A seal's life has much to recommend it. Much of the time is spent basking on a convenient rock or warm sandbank, and when it is hungry, the sea is full of fish.

An early illustration of the common seal, remarkable for its accuracy in depicting the dog-like head and tail.
G Rondoletius, 'De Piscibus', 1554

Killer whales are known to have taken seals off the coast of Britain, but their main enemy is salmon fishermen. Seals are protected by law in the breeding season and can only be taken outside it by a licence from the Department of the Environment, Food and Rural Affairs, DEFRA.

The UK population alone is said to be about 15,000.

'The way the bull seal expatiates upon his rock is delightful to see. Such great yawns, such stretchings, heavings and throwings back of the head, with supple curvings of the neck, such luxurious anticipation of repose to come – oh, such sleekness, such glistening. How intensely he enjoys this rest of his, his intertidal sleep. He was not asleep when we came, but now as he lies at length, tippling a little, with the waves that tipple round him, the eyes begin to close, and even when he throws back his head and opens his eyes, as he does often, they may be almost shut. Often he scratches his chin with his flipper or passes it indolently all over his face.'

Edmund Selous, birdwatcher in the Shetlands, 1905

GREY SEAL
(Atlantic grey seal)
Halichoerus grypus

Grey seals tend to prefer the most remote and isolated beaches, caves and storm-racked Atlantic coast islands. They are sea-going animals, completely at home in wild waves and on thunderous beaches. There are three separate populations. Those breeding in the Baltic and the western North Atlantic pup in early spring, on the ice, while our eastern North Atlantic animals come ashore much later. September in the Isles of Scilly, October in Ireland and Wales, November in Scotland. This British/Irish stock now constitutes something like half of the world population, so clearly it is an asset to be greatly valued.

The grey seals' breeding beaches are isolated either on islands or on the most remote mainland beaches, often exposed to storm conditions. Before and after the breeding season they tend to spend a lot of time in sociable gatherings, choosing undisturbed beaches

Length
bull 210–245cm
cow 195–220cm
Weight
bull 170–310ckg
cow 105–186kg

Cow grey seals basking. Engraving by James Stewart from Sir William Jardine 'The Naturalist's Library', 1839

where they lounge about and sleep a great deal of the day, interspersing this inactivity with bouts of play and fishing expeditions. It is at one of these assemblies that one is best able to distinguish the sexes. The bulls are generally more heavily built than the cows, and they have a greater breadth of muzzle and thicker necks, while the cows have a much straighter profile. Having said that, young bulls have more of the characteristics of cows, and old cows may look decidedly bullish. Although it is easy to say that bull seals may be sexed simply by their larger heads and generous roman noses, while the cow has a straight profile, in real life it is not so simple. Once they are ashore, the best method is to observe the tonal contrasts of the pelage, no matter what the general colour of the animal, which can be any combination of greys, browns and russets. If the seal's coat has light patches and spots on a dark ground, then it is a bull; if it has dark splotches and spots on a light ground, then it is a cow. This solves the problem of sexing the young bulls, which lack the roman nose, and old cows, which have a marked convexity of profile.

Pupping begins in the Isles of Scilly as early as the end of August, but the dates get later as you travel up the west coast; on the Welsh islands the peak period is the beginning of October, when there are pups of every age from newborn to a month old on the beaches. In Orkney and Shetland, seals pup in November.

Grey seals drop their pups, usually only one, but occasionally twins, well above the high-water mark in caves or at the back of a beach away from the reach of storm-driven tides, and the young seal normally stays put on land until it is a month old. At birth, when it is less than a metre long and weighs just over 13kg, it has a creamy, yellow-white coat of long hairs. Although at this stage it won't grow much in length, it soon becomes fat, fed with super-rich milk, and it grows from a skinny, white-coated pup to a barrel-shaped, grey-coated moulter in the space of 21 days. By this time it weighs nearer to 45kg, and is bloated with blubber. The cow will have stayed close by all this time, only going into the water if disturbed, but now she abandons it for good, going back to the sea and the waiting bull. The pup starves for a week or so before hunger forces it to sea and the first tentative efforts to find food, perhaps subsisting on crabs and whatever else it can forage till it perfects an inborn skill for pursuing more demanding prey. Seals feed mainly on fish, cod and salmon, which brings them into competition with fishermen, but also on cuttlefish and even the occasional bird.

Grey (top) and common seal heads

The first-year pups will travel fair distances, the Cornish, Irish and Welsh animals perhaps turning up in France, and the Scottish-bred seals visiting Norway; they face hard times and hard weather at first. Many succumb to storms, while many find themselves ashore on unsuitable beaches, where they are subject to well-meaning but misplaced attempts at rescue. In most cases they simply need a few hours' rest and sleep; quite the last thing they want is to be slung back into the sea!

Those that survive the early years return in due course to a sedentary and enviable life on their home coast.

'I am a man upon the land,
I am a selkie in the sea.
And when I'm far from every strand
My dwelling is on Sule Skerrie.'

The poem is related to the mermaid myth, and to the fact that, in the 19th century, Orkney men made yearly visits to Sule Skerry to collect two or three hundred seals 'for the purpose of eating, the inhabitants say they make good ham'.

WHALES

Whales, dolphins and porpoises are members of the order Cetacea. They are totally adapted to a life at sea but, as air-breathing mammals, they must surface to breathe. Modifications to the standard mammal design involve a hairless fish shape encased in a thick layer of insulating blubber, the nose on top of the head, forefeet becoming paddles, effective loss of hind feet and the tail becoming a horizontal fluke. Supported by water, they are free to grow to great size and weight. They are divided into two broad suborders: the Odontoceti (toothed whales) and the Mysticeti ('moustached' whalebone or baleen whales).

In diving, the blowholes are firmly closed and the heart-rate is slowed down. Whales are tolerant of a high concentration of carbon dioxide in the blood, with which they are plentifully supplied, the result being that they are able to hold their breath for periods that would drown land animals. The breathing passages are separated from the gullet so that they are able to feed underwater without choking.

Working in murky water and at great depths, toothed whales find their prey by echo-location, using ultrasonic pulses which are inaudible to human ears. They also communicate within their group with trills, whistles, grunts and groans which are perfectly audible to human ears above water.

Baleen whales have a profoundly different method of feeding. In relatively shallow water, they plough through the concentrations of plankton (possibly finding them by taste), gulping great quantities of water, expelling it through filter-plates of whalebone by contracting the ventral grooves of the throat and pressing the large tongue against the roof of the mouth, then swallowing the catch of uncountable numbers of small shrimps and larval fish. Not needing the agility and manoeuvrability of the hunting whales, they enjoy the advantages of greater size. The blue whale is the largest animal ever to live on earth, being 30m long and weighing 150 tonnes.

Records of whale strandings (which should be notified to the Receiver of Wreck at the nearest Custom House) have been kept by the British Museum (Natural History) since they were started in 1913, with a great deal of co-operation from the Coastguard and Receivers of Wreck. Over recent years the number of strandings has been increasing, for reasons which are not at all clear. Single whales may come ashore simply because they are sick and crave a superabundance of air, where they may be followed by others of their pod in a state of distress. Other possible reasons for mass strandings have been suggested. For instance, the whales may have chased a shoal of fish into the shallows, or their sonar systems may have become confused by navigational problems of narrow channels, shoals and bays.

Whales, though everyone knows they are mammals, are classified historically as Royal Fish, at least in the UK. As such, the stranded specimens are dealt with under the Wreck Regulations. Fishes Royal, which include sturgeon, belong to the Crown and are the prerogative of the monarch by ancient usage as a tithe rendered in exchange for guarding the seas and protecting the coast from pirates and robbers. They belong to the Crown not only when stranded but when caught in territorial waters. Although the practice dates back to Plantagenet times, the first record in the English language is of an Elizabethan lawyer who wrote in 1570 of

'greate or roialle fishe, as whales or such other, which by the Law of Prerogative pertain to the King himselfe'.

Edward I declared that in the case of a whale the King should have the head (the tongue being the delicacy), the Queen the tail and the captors the carcass. But Edward II made a clean sweep and proclaimed

'The King shall have wreck of the sea throughout the Realm.'

The putrefying remains of stranded cetaceans often pose local authorities considerable disposal problems, and it is as well for all of us that the Crown recognises responsibility for tidying them away. Mostly they are towed out to sea and sunk.

BRITISH WHALING

The history of whaling in northern Britain is largely that of the British/Norwegian company Salvesen of Leith. Most whales were caught north of Shetland, the catch consisting mainly of bottlenose, humpback, sperm and blue whales. But the industry was bedevilled from the start by the prejudices of consumers in Britain and on the Continent, who found it unpalatable.

The remains of a Hebridean whaling station are still to be seen today at Bunavoneader in North Harris. First established by Norwegians under licence by virtue of the Whale Fisheries (Scotland) Act, it was purchased by Lord Leverhulme in 1922 in pursuit of Lever Brothers' intention to corner all sources of whale oil from their competitors, but also because they felt they might improve the prospects for the important herring fishery. They suspected the Norwegians had been contaminating the local herring grounds with offal in the hope of driving the fish towards Norway! The station was never a financial success, and it finally ceased operation in 1951.

The International Whaling Commission (IWC) aims to regulate the harvesting of marine mammals. It is true that commercial whaling has an unhappy record of poor resource management and naked greed, but the challenge that has always faced the IWC is to monitor stocks and set quotas which are realistic enough to ensure a healthy future for whales.

Note: in the following species accounts, the length and weight measurements are only approximate.

WHALE WATCH

Report cetacean sightings to Sea Watch on 01865 727984 in the UK, or 01403 731679 in Ireland. Stranded whales should be reported to the local coastguard or the Receiver of Wreck at the Custom House or to the RSPCA on 09705 555999. For whale-watching around the coast of Britain and Ireland, check with the Whale and Dolphin Conservation Society, Alexander House, James St West, Bath BA1 2BT; tel: 01249 444224.

COMMON PORPOISE
(Harbour porpoise)
Phocaena phocaena

A stout and compact cetacean, the common porpoise has a short, blunt head without a beak. Grey-brown to black upperparts shade to grey and then white on the belly. A low and broad dorsal fin is set halfway down the back. Once common and widely distributed around our coasts, it is now markedly less so, found mostly off the west coast of Scotland, Orkney and Shetland.

The porpoise is an undemonstrative animal, lacking the exuberant leaping of some of the dolphins. It rarely shows much above the surface; mostly all you see is a glimpse of its dorsal fin and back as it surfaces – several times in a minute – for a blow in a slow roll. Porpoises tend to be heard rather than seen. Known as the 'puffing pig' in northern America (*Porcus piscus* in Latin, or pigfish) its blow is a characteristically explosive puff.

*Length
to 2m*

*Weight
to 60kg*

*'My father was
the keeper of the
Eddystone Light
And he slept with
a mermaid one
fine night.
Out of this union
there came three,
A porpoise and
a porky and the
third was me.'
Traditional folksong*

Porpoises are not particularly sociable, and are usually solitary or in small groups. Their diet consists primarily of fish such as mackerel or herring.

Common porpoises have been much persecuted in the past, but their present decline is less easy to explain. Many are caught in fishing nets, where they drown. They have shorter lives than most cetaceans, living to 12 if they are lucky.

GLOSSARY OF WHALE WORDS

Baleen Comb-like plates of bony material growing from the upper jaw of Mysticeti whales

Blow Moist air forcibly exhaled from the lungs through the nose (blowhole)

Breach To jump clear of the water's surface

Bubble-netting Behaviour associated with humpback whales, when they dive in a spiral, exhaling bubbles to enclose a shoal of pelagic fish which they then engulf from below, erupting explosively from the surface

Cetacean Member of the order Cetacea: whales, dolphins and porpoises

Dive pattern The typical sequence of dives and blows for a given whale species

Falcate Of the dorsal fin, meaning strongly curved or hooked

Fluke Propelling surface of a cetacean tail

Gam A sociable pod of gossiping whales

Lobtail Slapping the surface with a tail

Lunge-feed Of baleen whales, describes lunging along the surface in pursuit of plankton

Melon Bulbous forehead of toothed whales

Pod Group of cetaceans travelling together

Rostrum Upper jaw

Sound Diving to depth, as when the humpback reveals its tail

Spy-hop To poke the head vertically out of the sea

WHITE-BEAKED DOLPHIN
Lagenorhynchus albirostris

This animal has a robust body with a short beak. The beak, throat and belly are white, the forehead and back dark grey, and there are two conspicuous white patches on the flanks, seen as the animal rolls in breathing. It has a large and erect black sickle dorsal on the middle of its back.

Length 2.5–2.7m
Weight 200–300kg

White-beaked dolphins are gregarious animals, and are typically found in schools of hundreds. They are not especially agile, but may breach. They tend to bow-ride only for fast vessels. Their diet is mainly of cod, herrings and mackerel, but includes squid and some crustaceans.

They occur from Iceland to France and Portugal, associated with the edge of the continental shelf, but are most commonly found at the northern end of their range. Nevertheless they are the most common dolphins around the British Isles, being found off the west and northern coast of Scotland, but most often seen in the central and northern North Sea. Although they're most common in high summer, they can be seen in any month. Historically they escaped serious persecution and have not featured as captives in marine zoos.

ATLANTIC WHITE-SIDED DOLPHIN

Lagenorhynchus acutus

Length
2.7m
Weight
190kg

A robust animal, the Atlantic white-sided dolphin is slightly smaller than the white-beaked dolphin, with a short, thick, black beak, distinctly separated from the head by a groove. On the upperside it is black or dark-grey, a grey band seperating this from the white belly. There is a striking white/yellow oval blaze behind and below the dorsal fin, which is sharply curved back in sickle shape, and is tall and pointed.

These creatures are common in the northern part of the British Isles. Most often recorded on Orkney and Shetland, they are not uncommon in Scottish waters, especially west of the Hebrides. They are rare in the south.

White-sided dolphins tend to swim in large and lively schools, though perhaps this is less true of those in British waters. They are involved in much leaping, splashing and lobtailing. They are not enthusiastic ship-followers or bow-riders, but may be seen in close association with other dolphins and especially pilot whales.

Squid are an important item of diet, as are fish such as herrings and whiting.

Although still taken by harpoon in Norway, white-sided dolphins have escaped persecution in Britain.

DOLPHIN 'AUNTS'

Dolphin 'aunts' commonly assist in helping newborn infants to the surface for their first breath, but there have also been many accounts of dolphins coming to the aid of distressed individuals. Aristotle saw a dolphin supporting the body of a dead calf. More recently, a stunned animal was seen being supported by several of its fellows, who took it in turn to support it till it recovered. Classical tales of drowning poets being carried ashore on the back of a dolphin seem entirely credible.

COMMON DOLPHIN
Delphinus delphis

*Length
2m*

*Weight
80kg*

The quintessential dolphin, the common dolphin is sleek and streamlined; it has a well-defined black beak which may be white-tipped, and there is a dark circle around its eye. A distinct groove separates the head from the beak. The prominent and backward-curving dorsal fin is placed in the middle of the back. Chest and underparts are white and yellow in an hourglass effect which involves elaborate tan/mustard colourings on the flank. But a dark cape covers all, dipping below the dorsal to form a V-shaped saddle which is the most useful way of identifying the species.

Common dolphins are highly sociable and playful animals, confirmed bow-riders which may stay with a vessel for a long time, sometimes in large numbers, churning the sea and making a great deal of noise. They may join with other dolphins, for instance white-sided, when they are feeding. Sardines are a prime catch, but they also feed on cuttlefish and crabs from the bottom. At night, they will take squid which migrate up to the surface, but they may also dive down to 40m for squid, and have even been recorded down to 280m. The average dive is a couple of minutes, but it may run to eight minutes.

In other parts of the world they have been the subject of intensive exploitation, particularly in the Black Sea and in Japan. They are also the victims of by-catch in the tuna industry. Nevertheless populations seem to hold up. Stranded specimens show scars which suggest shark attack. Fortunately for them they are not amenable to training so are not exhibited in marine zoos. They are one of the most abundant species in deeper coastal waters, especially in the south and west of Britain and Ireland, mainly occurring between July and August, although they are less commonly seen off the east coast.

'They always swim in hilarious shoals which upon the sea keep tossing themselves to heaven like caps in a Fourth of July crowd.'
Herman Melville

A stranded common dolphin. Engraving by James Stewart from Sir William Jardine 'The Naturalist's Library', 1839

BOTTLENOSE
DOLPHIN
Tursiops truncatus

*Length
to 3m*

*Weight
to 200kg*

The bottlenose is a robust dolphin with a receding forehead and a distinct but fairly short beak. The lower jaw may have a white tip. The prominent dorsal is falcate (sickle-shaped) and placed halfway down the back. Colouring is subdued, being slate-grey or brown, with the throat and underside whitish to pink.

They tend to exist in small numbers, perhaps a dozen or so in a highly cohesive school. Mostly they are slow swimmers, but perfectly capable of spurts. As they roll over during breathing their backs are strongly arched.

Dives are in search of a variety of fish and crustaceans

and usually last about a minute. These dolphins may follow fishing boats to cadge fish disturbed by nets.

Schools tend to inhabit home waters on a seasonal basis, returning to their private fishing grounds year after year. They are widely distributed in the North Atlantic, are very common in English, Irish and Welsh coastal waters, and even in the Channel in summer months. They are also established seasonally in the Moray Firth of northeast Scotland.

Amenable to training for aquarium tricks, bottlenoses are the most familiar of zoo dolphins. In the wild, individuals not infrequently approach boats and become notorious as bathing and ball-playing companions, providing honest work for tripper boats. They may live in excess of 30 years.

The most familiar bottlenose dolphin in the British Isles is 'Fungi', who colonised Dingle Harbour in County Kerry in the mid-1980s and was still there well into 2002. Delighting many thousands of visitors, who have spawned a flourishing tripper-boat business, he cavorts shamelessly, on demand.

KILLER WHALE
(Orca, grampus)
Orcinus orca

Length
males to 9.5m
females to 7m

Weight
males to 7,000kg
females to 3,000kg

Killers are cosmopolitan and common, found in coastal areas throughout the seven seas. The largest of the dolphin family, their name has given them an undeservedly vicious reputation, so much so that there are those who try to sanitise them with the name 'orca'. However, this may invite even more confusion, since the Latin *Orcinus* means 'bringer of death', and *orca*, 'sea monster'. Killers they certainly are, taking birds, seals, fish (especially salmon) and, on occasion, other whales. There are no records yet of them taking tourists, though they are perfectly capable of overturning an ice floe in order to topple a sleeping seal into their jaws. They are commonly at home in British and Irish coastal waters, especially near seabird colonies and concentrations of seals.

The killer whale has a blunt head and is strikingly jet black above and brilliant white below, with a yellowy-grey saddle behind the dorsal fin, a diagnostic white ellipse behind and above the eye and a white incursion from the belly into the flanks behind and below the saddle. The dorsal fin is highly distinctive. In the female it is sickle-shaped and stands tall, but in the male it is triangular, reaching to almost 2m, and is unmistakable, even from a great distance.

Killer whale spy-hopping

Killers are curious and interested in ships. They are likely to change course and approach to cavort around and under a vessel which behaves with respect. They are lively creatures; although they don't bow-ride, they breach freely, lobtail, flipper-slap and spy-hop. They tend to travel in small family groups – pods – with a well-developed social structure, in which the dominant male is easily recognised by his tall fin. Pods may comprise anything from a few to a couple of dozen or more animals. A pod normally contains one dominant adult male and several breeding females, plus juveniles of both sexes – and it has a cohesive identity.

RISSO'S DOLPHIN
Grampus griseus

Length
to 4m

Weight
to 340kg

Grampus (a word more usually associated with the killer whale) is from the Latin, meaning 'a kind of whale'! Risso is from the amateur French naturalist, M Risso, who collected a stranded specimen from Nice in Provence in 1811 and sent the stuffed skin and skull to the famous anatomist Georges Cuvier, who classified it as *griseus* (grey), but wrote of it as '*le dauphin de Risso*' in such a way that Risso remains its vernacular name today.

Risso's dolphin has a bulbous head with no beak, a tall, dark, sickle-shaped dorsal set halfway down its back, long pectoral fins and a notched fluke. But its light grey, almost white, coloration, along with its often extensive network of scarring, is the easiest guide to identification. It is a deep-water dolphin of temperate waters, not infrequently seen within half a dozen miles of the British and especially Irish coast. In these waters, and mainly in summer, it is usually seen either alone or in small schools, often in the company of pilot whales. It may be confused with pilots but its head is not so conspicuously rounded and high. It certainly should not be confused with the beluga (white) whale, which has no dorsal fin. The marked scarring is presumably the result of altercations with others of its clan, since the toothmarks correspond to the spacing of the Risso's front teeth.

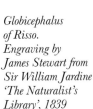

It is a fairly active animal, lobtailing, flipper-slapping and spy-hopping (see box on page 130) so high in the water that its flippers are out in the air, but it is not active by comparison with the common dolphin. It is most likely just to roll over at the surface. It is not a keen bow-rider, yet the famous Pelorus Jack, believed to be a Risso's, regularly bow-rode and shepherded ships through the Cook Strait of New Zealand for over 30 years in the early part of the 20th century. Blows occur every 15 or 20 seconds for three or four minutes, before a dive lasting from a few minutes to half an hour.

Little is known of its breeding arrangements. Its diet is mainly of cephalopods, such as squid and cuttlefish. It has not been subject to exploitation in our waters, but there is a Japanese fishery and some are taken in the Caribbean. It is not uncommon for Risso's to become stranded, usually in the south and west of the British Isles.

Globicephalus of Risso. Engraving by James Stewart from Sir William Jardine 'The Naturalist's Library', 1839

LONG-FINNED PILOT WHALE
(Pilot whale, pothead, blackfish, caa'ing whale)
Globicephala melaena

*Length
to 6m*

*Weight
males to 3 tonnes
females to 2 tonnes*

Pilot whales have a blackish body with a conspicuous bulbous forehead, also known as the 'pothead'. The dorsal fin is falcate (see box on page 130), while the flippers are long, sickle-shaped and pointed.

The name 'pilot' comes from their habit of swimming in line-astern, like a school crocodile. Traditionally fishermen believed that they would lead them to herring shoals.

They swim slowly, in compact schools of a few dozen or even many hundreds, and are common offshore in deep Atlantic water throughout the year, but they tend to visit coastal waters in pursuit of mackerel or herring shoals. Their main prey is squid and cuttlefish. In the Western Approaches, the west of Ireland and the north of Scotland they are not uncommon in any month, but can be seen mainly from June to September. At the turn of the year they may be seen further south. In the winter they may be seen in the North Sea.

In breathing, the bulbous head emerges first; the blow is strong, rising to nearly two metres. The roll is slow, almost all of the body rising above the surface before the animal submerges, to re-appear every couple of minutes. Most feeding dives are from 30 to 60 metres, but are possibly much deeper and last about ten minutes at a time. Although not particularly active (in fact they're often inclined to loaf about on the surface resting motionless), they may spyhop and lobtail (see box on page 130). They are not especially interested in ships, but may be tolerant of approach. They are not known to bow-ride.

Strandings, even mass strandings, are not uncommon, and in the event of an injured animal beaching itself a whole school may join it, a behaviour which has been worked to the advantage of fishermen. Fishermen of the northern isles, Orkney, Shetland and the Faeroes have herded inshore schools of 'caa'ing' (calling) whales to shallow bays, encouraging them by banging saucepans, throwing stones and generally creating mayhem until they beach themselves, to be harpooned, lanced or shot. To this day the Faeroese pursue pilot whales and slaughter them in the name of the traditional 'grind', a hunt which dates back at least to 1584. The catch seems stable, varying from a few hundred to a thousand or so every year. By contrast, Newfoundland stocks were over-exploited in the mid 1920s, but may now be slowly recovering under protection.

The deductor, or caa'ing whale. Engraving by James Stewart from Sir William Jardine 'The Naturalist's Library', 1839

HUMPBACK WHALE
Megaptera novaeangliae

Length
to 15m

Weight
to 48 tonnes

A cosmopolitan species, the humpback whale is found in all the oceans, ranging from the tropics to the edge of the polar ice. In the North Atlantic, one group is found from East Greenland to the Barents Sea, while the other migrates from the south of Greenland to breed in the Caribbean.

The humpback is a stoutly robust whale whose colour ranges from all-black to grey-to-black upperparts and white below. The small dorsal fin sits on a raised hump (hence the 'humpback') with a series of smaller bumps leading to the tail. The most striking feature is the extraordinarily long pectoral flippers, which can be nearly a third of the body length, or up to 5m long. The flippers are white or nearly white, and both they and the tail flukes are irregularly scalloped at the edges. The head, lower jaws and chin are covered with fleshy knobs, known as tuberosities.

Humpbacks cruise slowly, at four to six knots, but

they are powerful enough to leap clear of the water frequently in spectacular breaching. They normally blow half a dozen times, and not more than ten, at 15–30 second intervals on surfacing in a feeding session. In diving, their flukes rise high above the surface, revealing the pigmentation of the undersurface which is uniquely marked for each individual (in this way whale researchers can build up a photographic record for following their movements). Dives are for mostly less than 15, or maybe 20 minutes. They may occasionally 'lobtail', bringing the tail down explosively on to the surface, presumably as some form of warning display. They are highly vocal, whistling and rumbling musically in songs which are varied and intricate and clearly designed for long-distance communication. As baleen whales, they feed on crustaceans in the plankton. Their feeding technique is simply to engulf the swarms of krill, either just under the surface or by lunging up to them from below. (It is in Alaskan waters that they have perfected the 'bubble-feeding' method, where they swim in an upward spiral, corralling and concentrating small fish inside a curtain of bubbles.) Often, one of the long pectoral flippers rises above the water in one of the upward lunges, or when the animal is lounging at the surface.

Humpbacks normally breed every two years. After a 12-month gestation the single calf is born weighing a tonne and a half and measuring over 4m in length. They travel mostly in small groups, but may congregate in herds of a dozen or so. They are coastal animals, moving along predictable migration routes. Given that they are also slow-moving, this made them easy prey in the old whaling days, with the result that their world stocks are now sadly depleted and slow in recovery. There may be 2,000 in the North Atlantic, but they are seen only rarely in British waters.

Apart from man, their main enemy is the killer whale. They are usually infested with whale lice and host large numbers of barnacles.

Humpback whales have a bushy blow up to 3m high, and raise their tail flukes well above the surface before diving.

The underside of a humpback's tail fluke carries markings which identify the animal as an individual. If you are lucky enough to photograph the fluke, send a copy to Humpback Whale catalogue, Allied Whale, College of the Atlantic, Bar Harbour, Maine 04609, USA, with details of the date and the approximate position in which the whale was seen.

BLUE WHALE

Balaenoptera musculus

Length
to 30m

Weight
to 150 tonnes

The largest animal that has ever lived on earth – a grown adult is three double-decker buses in length – is called the blue whale because of its bluish-grey skin. *Musculus* is variously taken to mean 'muscular', which makes sense, or as a diminutive of the latin *'mus'* for mouse, which just may be an 18th-century Linnean joke.

The blue whale has a mottled, metallic-blue-grey body, a flat head, and a small, hook-shaped dorsal fin placed well back towards the slender and graceful fluke. It tends to be slow-moving, with a straight and powerful vertical blow – not bushy – which may reach nearly 10m high, especially in cold air. It generally breathes between shallow dives at 20-second intervals before diving for half an hour. After the spout, the long expanse of its back rolls over, the small dorsal emerging just before the tail fin makes a brief appearance. Surface cruising speed is about three or four knots (6–8km/h). They are easily spooked.

Blue whales travel alone or in groups of up to three or four, but may congregate at particularly rich feeding waters. In the Arctic summer they feed on krill, taking some 8,000kg in a day, which may amount to eight million shrimps.

When the pack-ice extends south at the onset of the Arctic winter, they in turn move south towards the warm tropical waters where they live off their blubber reserves and gather in discrete groups for courtship and mating at about ten years of age. The male's penis is over 3m long. The gestation period is nearly 12 months, so the single calves are born in the warm waters in which they were conceived. They are nursed for more than six months, by which time they are over 15m in length and they begin to take their share of the krill. They are sexually mature when they reach 23m in length. Females are thought to breed every three years.

Blue whales are widely distributed throughout the seven seas, both along shelf waters and the pack edge, and in open water. Their oceanic movements are little known. There are several discrete stocks, based in the North Pacific, the North Atlantic and the southern hemisphere. They are very rare visitors to British and Irish waters. Numbers were devastated by ill-regulated whaling in the 20th century, and progressively effective protection has so far failed to promote a real recovery. Their total world population may be in the region of 10,000. Their natural predators are gangs of killer whales which have been seen to attack blue whales, biting at their flukes and mouthparts.

'Leviathan… Upon earth there is not his like, who is made without fear. Will he speak soft words unto thee?'
Job 41

Greatest of all is the Whale, of the beasts which live in the waters,
Monster indeed he appears, swimming on top of the waves,
Looking at him one thinks that there in the sea is a mountain,
Or that an island has formed, here in the midst of the sea.
He also sometimes his hunger (which worries him often most greatly),
Wishes at once to relieve, warm is his wide open mouth,
Whence he then sends forth breaths of odours as sweet as the flowers.

Abbot Theobaldus of Monte Cassino, *Physiologus: A metrical bestiary*, c1022–1035

FIN WHALE
(Finback, razorback, common rorqual)
Balaenoptera physalis

Length to 27m

Weight to 90 tonnes

The second largest whale in the world, the fin whale was once common in the early part of the 20th century, but it is still a regular, spring and autumn passage migrant off the north and west coast of Britain and Ireland after its summer feeding time in Arctic waters.

The fin whale is similar in shape to the much rarer blue, but is smaller and has a larger dorsal fin (hence its common name). The rostrum (upper jaw) is also narrower and more V-shaped than that of the blue. It is dark-grey to brownish-black on the back and sides, the back being ridged from the dorsal fin to the flukes (hence the name 'razorback'). The underparts are white. Curiously, the head is dark on the port side and much paler on the starboard. Also on the starboard side the lower lip and baleen plates are yellowish-white while those on the port side are more blue-grey.

These irregularities are presumably connected with the way in which the animal scoops its plankton catch, when it rolls over on its side so that the starboard side becomes the under-surface and its mouth engulfs krill in a sideways fashion. It also deep-dives for fish and squid, reaching depths of over 230m.

In leisurely surfacing, the blow comes first – a tall and bushy spout spraying to six metres and blossoming at its full height – followed by a slow roll and the appearance of the dorsal fin, but not the tail. Four or five blows occur at intervals of 10–20 seconds, the final roll before the dive revealing more of the back and possibly the tail. In a deep dive the animal may be down for nearly half an hour.

Fin whales occasionally leap clear of the water in a breach. Often solitary, they may also travel in pairs or in small social groups. Fin whales are fast movers, able to cruise all day at a comfortable seven knots, but they can sprint at 18 knots, a speed which saved them from the attention of whalers until the arrival of fast catcher boats. When met in the open sea, they may choose to swim in company with a ship for a while, keeping station on the beam until they decide to fall back. Distribution of fin whales is worldwide, comprising three discrete populations. Those of the North Atlantic summer in the Arctic, moving south in late summer and passing Hebridean and southern Irish coasts to winter in warmer waters off the Iberian peninsula, even entering the Mediteranean.

Protected now, at least on paper, their numbers are probably increasing. There may be several thousand individuals in North Atlantic waters, but their total population is unknown.

Fin whale's dive sequence, showing the vertical blow, up to 6m. Tail flukes may not appear.

SEI WHALE
Balaenoptera borealis

Length
16m

Weight
12–15,000kg

The sei whale (pronounced 'say', the word deriving from the Norwegian *sejval*, or pollack whale) belongs to the family of rorquals, the biggest of which is the blue and the smallest of which is the minke whale. All have the throat grooves which extend from the lower jaw back behind the pectoral flippers and act in concertina style to allow the animal to swallow huge quantities of water and krill. The sei resembles a small

blue whale, but has
a relatively taller
hooked   dorsal
set two thirds back
on the body (further forward
than that of the blue or the fin).
They are dark bluish-grey, with a paler area associated
with the groove pleats. They may also have scars
inflicted by lampreys.

They tend to travel in small pods, perhaps only two
animals, perhaps half a dozen. The blow is a vertical
bush, reaching up to three metres, at 20 or 30 second
intervals, followed by a dive lasting five to
15 minutes, but mostly they feed on the surface,
skimming along rather than lunging. Their diet
consists mainly of plankton, krill or copepods, but also
includes small fish and squid. When they dive, it is a
subdued affair, the animal rolling over without arching
its back or showing its tail fluke.

Sei whales are widely distributed, except in polar
regions, but nowadays are rare, having suffered
greatly from over-enthusiastic hunting after the
stocks of blue and fin whales had been almost
exhausted. Northeastern Atlantic stocks summer in
the feeding waters of northern Norway, and may be
seen as passage migrants off the Hebrides and
western Ireland when they move to their wintering
quarters off Spain, Portugal and northwest Africa.

Oh, the lookout on the mainmast stood
With a spyglass in his hand.
'There's a whale, there's a whale, and a whale-fish,'
   he cried,
And she blows at every span, brave boys,
And she blows at every span.

Now the harpoon struck and the lines played out,
But she gave such a flourish with her tail,
She capsized our boat and we lost five men,
And we could not catch that whale, brave boys,
And we could not catch that whale.

'The Greenland Whale Fishery', folksong first recorded in 1725

MINKE WHALE
(Piked whale, lesser rorqual)
Balaenoptera acutorostrata

*Average length
males 8m
females 9m
(max length 10.7m)*

*Average weight
5,800–7,250kg
(max weight 9,000kg)*

The smallest and most abundant of the rorquals, with a streamlined but less slender body than its larger relatives, the minke whale has a narrow, pointed and triangular rostrum, with a ridge on top of its flat head. The upperparts are black, while the underparts are white from the chin back. There is pale grey blazing on the flanks, one above and behind the flippers and one in front of the fin. The tall, pointed dorsal fin is set well back on the body, and a pointed pectoral flipper sometimes has a striking white band across its middle in the northern population. They are often found close inshore.

Minkes are fast, dolphin-like swimmers, travelling on the surface at speeds of up to 16 knots. They are fairly commonly attracted to vessels, keeping station or even diving from side to side.

Their blow is low and insubstantial, and sometimes almost invisible; the animal often begins its blow before it has surfaced. Normally, the breathing sequence involves five to eight blows at intervals of less than a minute, followed by a dive lasting perhaps 20 minutes. The fin surfaces with the blow. On diving the tail stock is arched high, but the fluke does not appear. Sometimes they will breach clear of the water, occasionally many times in sequence.

Minke whales are seen as anything from single animals to several, but in areas of plankton abundance there may be a feeding assembly of hundreds. In feeding they may lunge many times in sequence, the entire head and most of the body coming out of the water. They take plankton and also squid. In turn they may be attacked by killer whales.

Minke males are sexually mature when they reach a length of about 7.2 to 7.7m, and females 7.9 to 8.1m, and are seven or eight years old. Gestation is 10–11 months, and the calves are weaned in six months. Migratory movements are little known, but they travel south to equatorial waters to avoid the boreal winter. Larger animals penetrate further north in the summer while non-breeders, calves and immatures remain further south.

The total world population may be in the order of a quarter of a million, leading to claims that exploitation is sustainable, but the northern population has suffered grievous over-exploitation in the past. They are fished by Norwegians, who claim the stocks are well able to withstand the harvest. Both economic considerations and public opinion will decide their future in the long-term.

Captain Minke was a Norwegian whaler who boasted of huge whales but actually captured small ones.

FURTHER READING
FIELD GUIDES

BIRDS

Bruun, B *Guide to the birds of Britain and Europe* Hamlyn (paperback), 1999

Elphick, J *Birdwatcher's Handbook* BBC, 2001. A highly recommended paperback, which includes an astonishing amount of basic information about bird identification, habitat, behaviour and movements.

Svensson, L *et al*, *Collins Bird Guide* Collins (hardback and paperback), 2001

WHALES

Carwardine, M *Whales, Dolphins, Porpoises* Dorling Kindersley, 2000

SEASHORE LIFE

Hayward, P *et al*, *Sea Shore of Britain and Europe* HarperCollins, 1996

ADDITIONAL READING

Birkhead, Tim *Great Auk Islands* T & A D Poyser, 1993

Bonner, Nigel *Whales of the World* Blandford, 1989

Brongersma, L D *British Turtles* British Museum (Natural History)

Carwardine, Mark et al *Whales & Dolphins* HarperCollins, 1998

Evans, P G H *Whales* Whittet Books, 1990

Fuller, Errol *The Great Auk* 1999

Hardy, Alister *The Open Sea* Collins New Naturalist, 1956

Harrison, Peter *Seabirds – an identification guide* Croom Helm, 1985

Hollom, P A D *The Popular Handbook of British Birds* Witherby

King, J E *Seals of the World* British Museum (Natural History)

Madge, Steve & Burn, Hilary *Wildfowl* Christopher Helm, 1988

Ogilvie, M A *Ducks* T & A D Poyser, 1975

Penhallurick, R D *Turtles off Cornwall, the Isles of Scilly and Devonshire* Dyllansow Pengwella, 1990

Ridgway, S and Harrison, R *Handbook of Marine Mammals* Academic Press, 1981

Sharrock, T *The Atlas of Breeding Birds in Britain and Ireland* BTO, 1976

Snow, D W & Perrins, C M *The Birds of the Western Palaearctic* OUP, 1998

USEFUL ADDRESSES

Bardsey Bird Observatory email: bob&lis@freeserve.co.uk

Marine Conservation Society 9 Gloucester Rd, Ross-on-Wye, Herefordshire HR9 5BU; tel: 01989 566017; fax: 01989 567815; web: www.mcsuk.org

The National Trust 36 Queen Anne's Gate, London SW1H 9AS; tel: 020 7222 9251; web: www.nationaltrust.org.uk. Owner of 600 miles of the British coast. Joining and supporting it is the most powerful way of demonstrating appreciation of its work.

Royal Naval Birdwatching Society Yachtsmen and merchant seafarers are encouraged to join and pool information by way of standardised recording methods. For more information contact Hon Secretary, Col P J S Smith RM, 19 Downlands Way, South Wonston, Winchester, Hampshire SO21 3HS

Royal Pigeon Racing Association The Reddings, Cheltenham, Glos GL51 6RN

Royal Society for the Protection of Birds (RSPB) The Lodge, Sandy, Beds SG19 2DL; web: www.rspb.org.uk

Seabird Group 14 St Vincent Rd, Tain, Ross-shire IV19 1JR; email: bob.swann@freeuk.com

Sea Watch Foundation 7 Andrews Lane, Southwater, West Sussex RH13 7DY; tel: 01403 731679

Whale and Dolphin Conservation Society Alexander House, James St West, Bath BA1 2BT; tel: 01249 444224

Wildlife Trust West Wales Welsh Wildlife Centre, Cilgerran, Cardigan SA43 2TB

'...though they be hid from my sight in the bottom of the sea,
thence will I command the serpent, and he shall bite them.'

Amos 9 v3

THE GREAT SEA SERPENT
(according to Pontoppidon)

The great sea serpent, Scoliophus atlanticus

INDEX

Main entries indicated
in **bold**, illustrations in *italic*

Alca torda 103
Alle alle 110
Allied Whale 145
Amos 160
Arion 133
auk,
   great **105**
   little **110**
auks 98
Aurelia aurita 12

Balaenoptera acutorostrata 152
B. borealis 150
B. musculus 146
Bardsey Island 41
Barents Sea 38
barnacle, acorn 16
barnacle, goose **16**, 26
Bass Rock 29, 47
Bempton 28
Beroe cucumis 15
Bewick, Thomas 39, 105
bill adaptations 99
bioluminescence 11
birds 24
blackfish 142
bonxie 76
Bridlington 29
British Museum
   (Natural History) 127
Bunavoneader 128

Cambrensis, Giraldus 27
Caretta caretta 22
Carew, Richard 114
catalogue, Humpback
   Whale 145
Catharacta skua 76
Cepphus grille 108
Cetorhinus maximus 2o
Chrysaora hyoscella 12
CITES 20
Clangula hyemalis 57
Clovelly 30
clown, sea 113
Columba livia 116

copepods 7, 150
cormorant **49**, *54*
Cormorants, Master of
   the 51
crustaceans 16
ctenophores 11, 15, *15*
Cuvier, Georges 140
Cyanea capillata 12

Darwin, Charles 11
DEFRA 122
Delphinus delphis 134
Dermochelys coriacea 23
Dingle Harbour 137
dinoflagellates 8
diver,
   black-throated *34*
   great northern *34*
   red-throated **32**, *33*, *34*
   white-billed *34*
divers 32
dolphin,
   Atlantic white-sided **132**
   bottlenose **136**
   common **134**, *135*
   Risso's **140**, *141*
   white-beaked **131**
dolphin 'aunts' 133
dovekie 110
Drake, Francis 106
Drayton, Michael 115
duck,
   eider **55**
   long-tailed **57**
ducks 55

eagle,
   sea 61
   white-tailed **61**
Eddystone Light 129
egg collecting 28
eider **55**
Eretmochelys imbricata 22
exploitation of coastal
   birds 26

faeces 110
Faeroes 38
Falco peregrinus 64
Farne Islands 56
finback 148
fish 19

Fisher, James 107
Fishes, Royal 127
Flamborough Head 29
foul gull 37
Fratercula arctica 113
Frohawk, F W 27
Fulmar 31, **37**, *37*
Fungi 137

Galway Bay 10
gannet 30, 31
   northern **46**
gannets and cormorants 45
garefowl 106
Gavia stellata 32
Gerard, John 27
goose, barnacle **27**, *27*
gooseberry, sea 15
grampus 138
Grampus griseus 140
Gray, R 61
grebe,
   black-necked *35*
   great-crested *35*
   little *35*
   red-necked *35*
   Slavonian *35*
Greenland Whale Fishery
   151
guano 52
gugas 30
guillemot **100**
   black **108**
gull,
   black-headed 28, **79**
   common 84
   great black-backed **87**
   herring **82**
   lesser black-backed **85**
   Sabine's 90
gull, derivation 81
gulls 78

Hakluyt, R 107
Haliaetus albicilla 61
Halichoerus grypus 123
Hardy, Sir Alister 14
Hawkins, Richard 106

Innocent III, Pope 27
International Whaling
   Commission 128

157

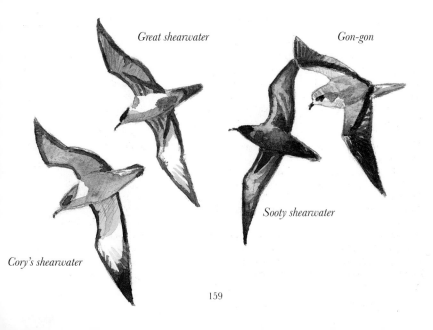

Great shearwater

Gon-gon

Sooty shearwater

Cory's shearwater

AUTHOR

Tony Soper first saw the light of day and the sea from his father's wharf on the Cattewater in Plymouth. First tentative days in pulling boats in the Sound were followed in due course by a succession of ancient gaffers and a 50-ton passenger vessel with which he encouraged day-trippers to enjoy the wildlife of the coast of Devon. More recently he pioneered wildlife cruising in expedition ships and Russian research vessels around the coast of Britain and Ireland, to say nothing of summering in both theArctic and the Antarctic, chasing the Arctic tern in pursuit of perpetual summer. As a naturalist and wildlife film-maker, he co-founded the BBC's now-famous Natural History Unit. He holds the Board of Trade's Yachtmaster ticket and the Master Diver ticket from the late and much-lamented British Underwater Centre. He is President of the Stugeron fan club.

ILLUSTRATOR

Dan Powell has been a wildlife artist since graduating from Dyfed College of Art in Wales in 1983. He was honoured as *British Birds* Bird Illustrator of the Year in 1996. His work has appeared in numerous books and journals, including *The Arctic: A Guide to the Wildlife*, also published by Bradt Travel Guides, and many publications by the Royal Society for the Protection of Birds on subjects ranging from parrots to dragonflies. He is happiest when out sketching in the field – especially when stuck in the middle of a bog.

ACKNOWLEDGEMENTS

This book owes much to Ronald Lockley, who took me as unpaid deckie-learner on joyous seal and seabird-ringing trips along the wonderful coast of west Wales. And to Trevor Hampton, who improved my seamanship and taught me to dive and explore the underwater coast of Devon. More recently I want to acknowledge the friendship and trust of a number of shipmasters, including Karl-Ulrich Lampe of MS *Hanseatic*, Sergey Paschov of MV *Alle Tarasova*, Sergey Nesterov of RV *Professor Multanovskiy*, Filip Kolesnikov and Gennady Josephov of RV *Professor Molchanov*. Professional seamen like to stay well clear of rocks, shoals ands shelves; naturalists like to pass the time of day with them. Seamen who can straddle both worlds and keep their sense of humour are worth knowing!

Too many naturalists have struggled to keep me on the straight and narrow to name here, but I have been lucky to sail with Sir Peter Scott, Morton Boyd, Roger Lovegrove, Dr John Sparks, Anna Sutcliffe, Dr Kim Crosbie and Professor David Nicholls, and want to thank them for their inspiring company.

T S

It takes a certain sort of maniac to want to spend time looking at an empty sea in the hope that something fantastic is going to pass by. So I would like to acknowledge all those folks with whom I have passed the time away in this pursuit – in particular Mike Wearing, who is definitely a 'certain sort of maniac'.

DP